MALCOLM DEACON

The Church
on
CASTLE HILL

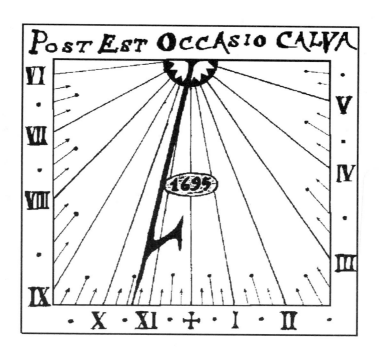

the history of
**Castle Hill United Reformed Church,
Northampton**

Park Lane Publishing
1995

The Church on Castle Hill

the history of
Castle Hill United Reformed Church
Northampton

Published by Park Lane Publishing
Tel: 01604 858363

Design by Cloverleaf Publications
Tel & Fax: 01604 821560

Photography by Charles Ward Photography Earls Barton
Tel: 01604 812465

Printed by Kingsley Press
Tel: 01604 497778

Preface, notes on sources and acknowledgements

The purpose of this book is to trace the history of a Christian fellowship that has held together in the faith over three centuries. It is a story that commences in the dark days of persecution in the 17th century when men and women were obliged to worship where they could; increasing freedom gave them the opportunity to build their own Meeting House on Castle Hill. There, successive generations have continued to worship God and serve the community around. The book is full of personalities, both ministerial and lay, who have made an impact upon the life of the church and the town. There are many names not mentioned simply due to the limited space available, but they are not forgotten as each individual is known by God. In a real sense the story that is told is uncompleted as the church moves faithfully on. This book sets out to record the main features of that history within a changing society and urban landscape. Whether it is the growth of freedom to worship in the 18th century, the urge to provide Sunday Schools for the growing population in the nineteenth, or the impact of world wars, urban demolition and social disillusionment in the twentieth, the church has nevertheless continued in its faithful task.

In the main, this volume seeks to break new ground by publishing information previously unknown or difficult to obtain; this is particularly true regarding illustrations, many of which are published for the first time. The scholarly apparatus of footnotes and references is deliberately kept to a minimum, although pathways into the recorded historic data are indicated for the serious student; a select bibliography is included. Time and space forbid an index. Earlier histories of the church by T. Arnold & J. J. Cooper (1895), and Bernard S. Godfrey (1947) have been consulted. Manuscript sources, namely an unpublished *Continuation of the History of Castle Hill 1895 - c1920* by H. N. Dixon, the history of the Sunday School *The Story of a Century* by John Archer, plus numerous other uncatalogued documents and papers have been studied. Also the original deeds of the church, many on parchment have been closely scrutinised for the first time in at least a century. It was whilst studying these sources that previously unpublished letters of Dr Doddridge were discovered. Material on Commercial Street Congregational Church is largely obtained from the centenary volume (1929) by S.S. Campion *A Chapter in Local Religious History.*

For the purposes of this book the terms *Dissenter* and *Nonconformist* are used synonymously, although there is an historic difference. *Dissenter* was first used after the Restoration to describe those who would not conform to the restoration of bishops in the Established Church. *Nonconformist* originated in the reign of Elizabeth I and referred to Puritans who would not conform to the *Prayer Book* of 1559. Only after the Great Ejectment of 1662 did *Nonconformist* come to mean separation. By the second half of the 19th century the term *Dissenter* was virtually replaced by *Nonconformist;* this in its turn gave way to *Free Churchman* in the 20th century.

Grateful acknowledgement is made to Barbara Reeves for extremely valuable assistance with the research for the book, especially for background material on the immediate area of the church. Grateful appreciation is also given to Charles Ward Photography. Thanks, too, to Colin Lindsay for the sketch and the material on the sundial, to Bernard & Joan Jeffery for a scrapbook of press cuttings, to the Revd Laurie Wooding and Roy & Joyce Embrey for advice on the history of Commercial Street and its amalgamation in 1959. Also thanks to Roy for his plan of the Castle Hill Church showing the stages of development of the building. I express my grateful thanks for the privilege of being able to write this history for the church's Tercentenary. It is to the present generation of Christ's followers, as well as to those who have gone before us and those who will come after us that this book is dedicated.

Malcolm Deacon. Northampton. June 1995.

Contents

Abbreviations within the text:

AC	=	*The History of the Church of Doddridge and Reminiscences* by Arnold & Cooper.
BG	=	*Castle Hill Meeting* by Bernard Godfrey.
HND	=	*Continuation of the History of Castle Hill* by Hugh Neville Dixon.
PDN	=	*Philip Doddridge of Northampton* by Malcolm Deacon.
TG	=	*A History of Castle Hill Church* by Thomas Gasquoine and others.

Part 1 The Historic Background

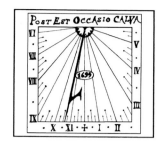

Castle Hill

Early in the fifth century the civilisation established in Britain by the Romans began to crumble under the pressure of warlike tribes from the continent of Europe. Administration was destroyed as were the outward signs of Roman rule: towns and villas were left unrepaired, became abandoned and trade and commercial activity became almost impossible. Yet by the mid sixth century some order was being fashioned out of the chaos with the establishment of kingdoms such as Kent, Mercia and Northumbria. Towards the close of that century, in 594, Christianity came to England with the landing of St Augustine on the shores of Kent.

On a low hill facing south and west, close to the River Nene and adjacent to the pre-Roman (Iron Age) routeway of the Jurassic Way the Anglo Saxons established (c700) a small settlement. With ample supplies of water, good pasturage on the alluvial soils of the upper Nene Valley the site was ideal for farming. Thus *home farm* or *ham tun* was commenced, the beginnings of Northampton. The settlement grew using the curve of the river as its southern and western defensive line and to the north a timber revetted earthen bank was constructed with outer and inner roads. On the knoll overlooking the river a wooden church was constructed which indicated that the site had a degree of stability and importance in these troubled times. It is known that the missionary, Bishop Wilfred, was active in the area and might have been instrumental in its establishment. The church, which was later rebuilt with stone in the Norman period, is now known as St Peter's. In these early times it possibly functioned as the chapel to the Saxon lord or even royal owner of the estate.

The Saxon settlement enclosed some 60 acres, and around St Peter's church a small town had emerged with single storey timber framed buildings. Iron smelting and working were undertaken as was weaving. Close by in the area now known as Chalk Lane other buildings appeared especially a timber hall which was reconstructed in the eleventh century. Archeological finds such as slag from metal working, pottery including *Northampton ware* and from further afield (even the continent) indicate that Hamtun was a busy place in the late Saxon period. The axis of the town was in the crossroads formed by the east/west track (marked today by Marefair/Gold Street) which crossed a major branch of the ancient Jurassic Way (now Horse Market/Horseshoe Street).

Life dramatically changed with the coming of the Normans who not only trod England down but trod it into a new shape. The impact upon the town was traumatic with local Saxons forced into the construction of a huge civil engineering project ordered by William the Conqueror and supervised by the first Earl of Northampton, Simon de Senlis. As Northampton sat astride the major route between the northern capital York and the southern capital Winchester, and the east/west route between East Anglia and the Welsh Marches it was vital to construct a fortress from which the Normans could centre an army to subdue all resistance. Thus a castle was built at the south western part of the town using the river for defense and spreading on to the Chalk Lane site the highest part of the settlement, *Castle Hill*. At the same time the town itself was extended to some 245 acres behind stone walls constructed by the reluctant Saxons. By the time the Domesday Book was completed in 1086 the town comprised some 300 houses which suggests a population of up to 2000 people and was taxed at £30.10s one of the top twenty boroughs in the kingdom. A considerable number of French settlers had established themselves within the new town. By the late twelfth century Northampton was one of the six most wealthy towns in the land.

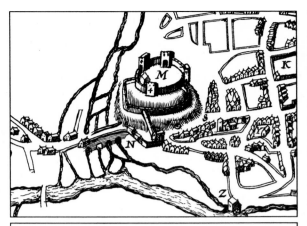

Portion of the Map of Northampton by J. Speed, 1610.

The castle functioned as a focal point for royal visitations and religious and parliamentary councils. Here much legislation was enacted and six General Church Councils met between 1136 and 1266; and at the Council held in 1164 Thomas a Becket was put on trial. Yet Northampton failed to become the capital of England; the shift in national preoccupation from internal security to the war in France together with the rise of London left the town to begin a steady decline which continued throughout the Middle Ages. The castle began to decay and eventually proved to be uninhabitable. By the time of Elizabeth I it was badly dilapidated, and during the time of Charles I sheep were being grazed within its walls. During the Civil War a Commonwealth garrison was stationed there, and in 1642 and again in 1645, following the Battle of Naseby, it was used as a temporary prison. Castle Hill or *Castle Hills* became a place of some desolation, adjacent to the former castle orchard and cherry garden and close by the medieval church of St Mary's. This church was built by the Dominicans in 1235 and was enlarged during the next century; in 1338 the Royal Chancery was established in the church which eventually was demolished in 1539 at the Dissolution.

On 20 September 1675, in St Mary's Street, close to Castle Hill a domestic fire broke out which, assisted by a strong westerly wind, soon engulfed the thatched roofs and timber frames of the nearby cottages. A major part of the town was completely destroyed including All Saints Church. In the following years the rebuilding of the town proceeded apace with wider streets and buildings of stone and brick instead of wood and thatch. Yet Castle Hill remained unaffected bounded by the remains of the castle on the west and a few cottages on the east which had survived the Great Fire. The map drawn by John Speed in 1610 shows the castle complete with motte and bailey dominating the town with a cluster of houses close by to the east and, to the south, St Peter's Church surrounded by houses. On the east, north and west faces of the hill there was open ground. During the Civil War further rubble was heaped there making it yet higher in order to place cannon strategically at its summit, particularly to cover the castle gate. It is possible that houses to the south of the hill were demolished during 1642-3 in order to give a clear line of fire towards the London Road and Hardingstone. A more accurate survey by G. Nunns in 1743 for the land owner at that time, Sir Arthur Heselrigge, shows the actual site of the castle within the walls of the *young orchard* with Chalk Lane abutting on to the *upper roundabout*, a one and three quarter acre grass grown moat, and the bank between the moat and the castle walls. The Noble and Butlin survey of 1746 shows Castle Hill as a distinct knoll together with the Meeting House to the south and reached by Chalk Lane and Quart Pot Lane. To both west and north there are no buildings, and Castle Lane leads down to the River Nene at the foot of the hill.

For many years the old castle had been a useful quarry for ready cut stones. The *Castle Hills* had become a general wasteland strewn with rubble and dung. Close by was the old St Mary's graveyard with vestiges of its walls which ran part of the length of Chalk Lane. Derelict, burnt out properties, namely `two messuages, houses or tenements...late in the tenure or occupation of Widow Golby and Thomas Mawbut' and owned

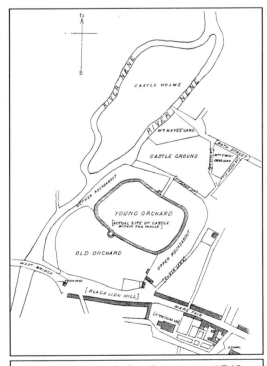

Survey of Hesilrige Property, 1743.

by the orphaned Joyce Talbot aged fourteen, were being offered for sale on her behalf by Thomas Warner of Daventry. It was this undesirable property that attracted the eyes of the Dissenting church fellowship who were seeking land on which to build a meeting house in which they could worship unmolested and without attracting attention. Away from the hub of the town's life the Dissenters wanted to practise their faith in peace and tranquility. The past thirty years had had too many painful memories for them and they looked with hope and faith towards a more tolerant and pleasant future.

In 1695 Thomas Dust (hatter, of Northampton), Richard Pendred (currier, of Northampton), William Burkitt (yeoman, of Bugbrooke), John Buswell (yeoman, of Duston), Robert Chambers (gentleman, of Northampton), John Sanders (currier, of Northampton), George Mason (shoemaker, of Northampton) and Thomas Rabbitt (grocer, of Little Houghton) took the bold step of paying £26 in good lawful English gold for the property. On 3 May the site was conveyed to the church representatives; the conveyance deed witnesses that they received:

'all that toft, piece, plot or parcel of ground whereon the said houses or tenements lately stood...all which premises were situate in the parish of St Peter's in the Town of Northampton between St Mary's Churchyard there on the South side thereof and a great Dung-hill or place of rubbish on the North side thereof, together with all outhouses'.

Cheered by their acquisition of land they proceeded with alacrity to clear the ground and build their Meeting House.

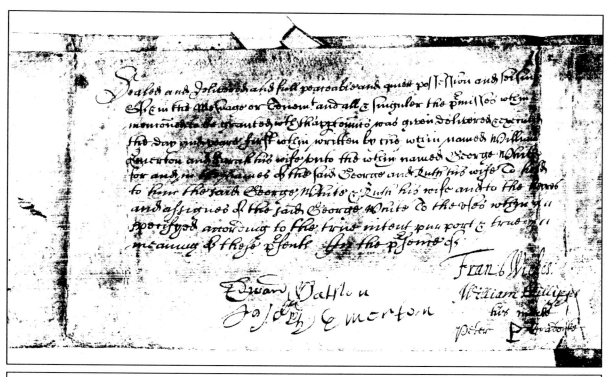

The earliest document in the church's possession.
A conveyance of property dated 30th September 1665, ten years before the Great Fire of Northampton and thirty years before it was purchased for the erection of the Meeting House.

The Dissenters

As Thomas Dust and his companions began to clear the ground and lay the stones for the Meeting House they were acutely aware of the progress which it signified. Only thirty-three years previously an act of parliament, *the Act of Uniformity*, had been passed which sought to root out from the Church of England (the Established Church) all forms of Puritanism. Every incumbent of the established church was ordered to declare his 'unfeigned Assent and Consent to all and everything contained and prescribed' by *the Book of Common Prayer*. It was an ultimatum which, on St Bartholomew's Day (24 August 1662), forced more than two thousand clergy, lecturers and fellows of colleges from their posts. Unable to collect their annual tithes many were plunged into immediate poverty. Driven from the towns, fined, pilloried, imprisoned and harassed many were faced with utter misery and destitution.

The Great Ejectment, as this deliberate act of persecution became known, failed in its object. Ministers and people had hardened their resolve in the teeth of fierce opposition. The political, social and educational influence of all Dissenters had been assailed by *the Clarendon Code*, a fistfull of penal laws: *the Corporation Act* (1661), *the Act of Uniformity* (1662), *the Conventicle Act* (1664) and *the Five Mile Act* (1665). Under the first of the new laws no Dissenter could hold public office unless allegiance to the King was sworn and holy communion according to the rites of the Church of England was taken. Dissenters lost their seats on borough councils and some were even elected in order for them to be fined for refusing to comply with the regulations. Much injustice resulted from *the Conventicle Act* under which informers claimed up to a third of the goods from Dissenters' estates; many lost all their belongings and even the tools and materials of their trades. In 1673 *the Test Act* reached the Statute Book denying naval, military and civil employment to Dissenters. They were treated with insolence, cruelty and perfidy. Congregations were scattered and individuals found themselves pilloried, fined, imprisoned or even banished from the country. Many died being transported to the colonies, and meetings were broken up and the worshippers beaten up and abused with indecent savagery.

The Dissenters had to devise devious stratagems in order to escape detection. Times and places of worship were often changed and trap doors were constructed so that preachers could escape or hide when necessary. Adjacent houses even had secret passages dug or walls removed. Ingenuity went so far as to ask worshippers to provide bread and cheese so that their services, if disturbed, could be instantly turned into convivial gatherings. Scores of *Free Churches* date from the period of *the Great Ejectment*; it is from this crisis that organised Nonconformity emerged, fusing together the Puritan stream from within the Established Church and the Separatist movement from without. The overthrow of James II in 1688 and the accession of William of Orange to the English throne led to an increased liberty for Dissenters. In the following year the Toleration Act was passed which granted to all Nonconformists a limited right to dissent in forms and ceremonies of worship, although they were not at liberty to dissent from the doctrines of the established church, especially the doctrine of the Trinity. In recognition for swearing an oath against Papal rule and supremacy Dissenters were exempted from the Elizabethan laws which compelled them to attend their parish churches. Although they had no difficulty in complying with the mandate to attend worship each Lord's Day other impositions remained. They had to pay tithes and church rates and their meeting houses had to be certified before the Bishop of the diocese, his Archdeacon, or a Justice of the Peace. Dissenting preachers and teachers, under pain of punishment under *the Clarendon Code*, had to subscribe to most of *the Thirty Nine Articles*. Dissenting ministers remained unable to serve as jurors, churchwardens or overseers. Failure to take the oaths required was met with instant imprisonment without bail.

As the Northampton Meeting House neared its completion in the autumn of 1695, built with the russet coloured stones which lay in profuse heaps in the vicinity (ruins of the old castle, the town walls and rubble from other buildings destroyed in *the Great Fire* of 1675) the builders could reflect with gratitude that they had at least a measure of freedom in which to worship God as they desired. Under *the Toleration Act* the Established Church, although it held exclusive political and educational power, had lost much of its power to persecute. The Dissenters were content with the improvements made and were anxious to proceed apace with their building work. Experience had taught them to grasp every opportunity as it presented itself. In 1672 a temporary *Indulgence* had granted Dissenters a chance to obtain preaching licences yet within a year it was cancelled and all licences recalled in 1675. This temporary respite, however, had given them a vital boost to their confidence and a chance to make some progress.

Title page of a Bible, once in the ownership of the Doddridge family. Printed by R. Field for the Parliament 1653. It measures only 4 x 2 x 1.5 inches.

Northamptonshire had long been a centre of religious dissent even before the watershed of 1662 dissenting congregations had arisen. Soon after 1645, a climactic year that witnessed the Battle of Naseby, Presbyterian, Congregationalist and Baptist congregations were formed. In Northampton Dissenters from St Giles Church and St Peter's Church formed themselves into a Presbyterian church, and it is generally accepted that the ejectment of the Rev Jeremiah Lewis from St Giles in 1662 was a vital catalyst in encouraging Dissenters to meet for worship in barns and houses. By 1674 this Presbyterian Church was in vigorous existence, resisting the inroads of the powerful evangelising efforts of the Independent Church at Rothwell founded in 1655 and which resulted in the establishment of the church which is now College Street Baptist Church. Yet a third group formed a Strict Baptist Church which met on The Green close to St Peter's.

Gradually the disparate Presbyterian groups began to find points of focus, places in which to meet and leaders around whom to gather. In Northampton Richard Hooke M.A., ejected in 1662 from his living as Rector of Creaton, preached for a short time in the village, where he opened a school, before preaching in his own house in Northampton. He later moved to another property bounded to the south by Osborne's Jetty that straddled the Drapery and Market Square. Hooke gained a licence as a Presbyterian minister. He died in 1679 and is buried in St Peter's Church which, in his lifetime, he frequently attended. Another Presbyterian preacher was John Harding, ejected from his livings at Ambrosden, Oxfordshire and Melksham, Wiltshire. He died in 1690 and his memorial in St Peter's Church describes him as a `Minister of Jesus Christ'. His father, another John Harding, likewise ejected in 1662 from his living at Brinkworth, Wiltshire, is also buried at St Peter's Church. That such men could find a safe haven in Northampton in which to express their religious convictions says much of the relatively tolerant atmosphere in the town. Presbyterian worship was conducted in the homes of John Clarke, Valentine Chadock, Samuel Wolford (or Welford), Alexander Blake and the barn and house of Robert Massey (Marsey or Marley) who was a lawyer. Wolford, whose house was licensed for Presbyterian teaching, was one of the early members of the Castle Hill Meeting and it seems clear that the building of the Castle Hill Meeting was the essential means of bringing these groups together as one congregation.

The Great Fire of 1675 destroyed some licensed preaching places, notably Richard Hooke's house in the Drapery and Robert Massey's in the Chequer (Market Square). Alexander Blake's house in St Martin's (Broad Street) possibly escaped and Massey's barn survived. There are no records as to the fate of the other known preaching places. Although the exact locations of the meeting places for the Presbyterians prior to 1695 one piece of evidence focusses attention on the activities of John Clarke, a draper and prominent citizen, having been Chamberlain in 1687 and Mayor in 1691-2 and a staunch Presbyterian. The Diary of Thomas Isham of

Lamport records Clarke as `preaching and building a house', and it is known that he had purchased *the Swan Inn* situated in the Drapery sometime before *the Great Fire*. In 1677-8 the Fire Court ordered him to rebuild his property, and it is not beyond possibility that *the Swan Inn* was an early meeting place of the Dissenters. One thing is certain, however, and that is the sentiment expressed on the new meeting house's southern exterior. High on the wall the builders had placed a sundial with the Latin motto `Post est occasio calva'; derived from the Roman poet Cato, `opportunity has locks before, but behind is bald'; it is a poignant reminder that it is necessary to grasp the hair of opportunity whilst he is in front of you otherwise one's fingers will slip off his retreating bald head.

Sketch of the Meeting House.
To the south is St Peter's Church and to the west lies the castle moat.

Part 2 Early Ministries:
Blower, Shepard, Hunt and Tingey

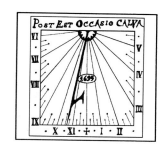

Revd Samuel Blower: 1672? to 1694

The arrival in Northampton of the Rev Samuel Blower was to be the vital catalyst in bringing together the various Dissenting groups within the town. Like Hooke and Harding he had been ejected from his living in 1662. A man of considerable academic ability Blower had been dismissed from his Fellowship of Magdalen College, Oxford in 1660; two years later he was forbidden to preach at Woodstock where he had held the living since 1657. Subsequently he had been private chaplain to Samuel Dunch of Baddesley, Hampshire and in 1672 had been licensed as a Congregational general teacher at Sudbury in Suffolk. Although it is not possible to date Blower's arrival in Northampton with any accuracy (the earliest speculation being in 1672) it is certain that he was active in the town in 1690. He had been a contemporary of Harding at Magdalen College and the two had worked closely together during the later years of the Protectorate in Oxfordshire. It is most likely that Harding's influence attracted Blower to Northampton where he probably ministered to a group of Christians with Congregationalist sympathies meeting in Massey's barn. It is unlikely that he co-pastored the group meeting in Harding's house. The latter was of strong Presbyterian views, the son of `a most violent Presbyterian'. Blower was of a different temperament and described as `a man of meek temper, peaceable principles, and a godly life'.

1690/91 was a time when Presbyterians and Congregationalists `in and about London' were making strenuous efforts to co-operate. How far this *Happy Union* influenced Northampton is not known although the death of Harding provided Blower with the opportunity to unify the disparate groups within the town into a single Nonconformist Church. The *Great Fire* had forced groups of similar persuasions together out of simple necessity. `Blower was able to carry this unifying process a stage further and unite in one Church all Nonconformists irrespective of denomination' (BG13). Blower's personality was such that many were attracted to him: his non-pompous style of preaching, a friendly disposition, a caring attitude to those in trouble, an interest in young people, and a prayerful concern for all formed a distinct spiritual tone in the Church.

Blower was able to protect the newly emergent church from the dangers of the times. `Mr Blower was as well suited to the times as to the people. A bolder man would have exposed them and himself to greater perils. A more timid would not have had enough courage to cope with the difficulties and dangers of his office'.(AC42). One major problem encountered by Blower and other ministerial colleagues was the fervent evangelism of Richard Davis, the congregational minister at Rothwell. Davis's activities were seen as `a dismal plague...begun at Rowell'. His outspokenness, use of lay preachers and evangelists who made inroads into other ministers' territories caused much offence. Davis' church admitted into membership people from no fewer than 140 places in Northamptonshire and five neighbouring counties. Several members lived in Northampton and friction began to grow over the Rothwell church's uncertainty that Blower's church was `a church rightly constituted and that they own this as a true church of Christ'.

In the autumn of 1692 Blower joined with other ministers at an assembly in Kettering bringing to a head the complaints that Davis and his preachers had `set up Meetings...in or near the places where dissenting Ministers have their stated congregations and churches'. Blower alleged that such a situation existed in Northampton bringing with it a threat to the unity which had been built up. There is no doubt that such dissension resulted in a withdrawal of members of Blower's church, mainly those who joined with those who advocated `Baptism on Profession of Faith' and who centred their activities upon Lady Fermor's house in Bridge Street. This congregation became enchurched in 1697, two years after the building of the Castle Hill Meeting. This was to become the College Lane Church under the ministry of its pastor, John Moore. A careful comparison of the earliest names of the College Lane and Castle Hill church books reveals that at least sixteen persons who were members of Castle Hill in 1694 or shortly afterwards eventually transferred membership to College Lane.

It therefore seems clear that for a brief period in the early 1690's a Nonconformist church existed in Northampton under the pastoral care of Samuel Blower; this was to become the Castle Hill Church. Its basically Presbyterian church order led to those impatient of ecclesiastical restraints, and also those who held the principle of believer's baptism rather than infant baptism, to separate from it. Nevertheless, when Blower left Northampton in 1694 for Abingdon, Berkshire (where he died in 1701) he left a strongly united body of one hundred and sixty-four to call his successor.

Revd Thomas Shepard: 1694-96

After a call to prayer the church sent a `Unanimous Call' to the Revd Thomas Shepard to succeed Mr Blower `in the Pastoral Office'. Like his father Shepard had been an Anglican clergyman. He had felt it necessary to withdraw from the established church having had differences of opinion with his Bishops in his livings at St Neots and later Haversham, Buckinghamshire. He moved to Oundle to join his father, who was pastor of the Congregational church there, before coming to Northampton in 1694 at the age of twenty-nine. He consented to the Call insisting that his ministry in Northampton should be conditional upon minister and people consenting to `walk comfortably together in all the ways and Ordinances of the Lord'.

Shepard was a man of great piety and expected similar devotion in all members of the church. He drew up a Church Covenant insisting that all members sign it:

`We this Church of Christ whose names are underwritten, having given up ourselves to the Lord and one to Another according to the Will of God, do promise and Covenant in the presence of God, to walk together in all the Laws and Ordinances of Christ according to the Rules of his Gospell thro' Jesus Christ so strengthening us'.

Furthermore, throughout 1695 and 1696 Shepard moved the church to agree procedures for the admission of new members. Those wanting to join the church had to give testimony and prove themselves serious and worthy in their candidature as church members; enquiries by the church would need to take time in order `to enquire into the conversation of the said persons'.

On 4 October 1694 the church appointed Thomas Dust and Richard Pendred `to execute the Office of Deacons and they manifesting their acceptance of the Call were accordingly...fully enstated or empowered by the Churches Act'. Clearly, the church was making the most of *the Toleration Act* of 1689 that hoped to bring `some ease to Scrupulous Consciences in the Exercise of Religion'. Shepard had arrived in Northampton only six months before the Castle Hill site became a scene of intense activity. The *Church Book* is silent as to the building of the Meeting House and we are left to imagine the strenuous efforts that were made to complete the construction before the winter set in late in 1695.

Nothing is known of the official opening services of the Meeting House. The *Church Book* records that on 3 October 1695: `It was agreed that Brother Owen should look after the Meeting House; that his work should be to sweep it weekly and open and shut it every Lord's day, for which six pence should be his weekly allowance at present'. Owen evidently gave good service as a later entry dated 4 April 1701 reads: `A Greed that John Owen should have 10 shillings for looking after the Meeting every quarter'. (Bernard Godfrey wondered whether the first two words of the sentence were a deliberate pun).

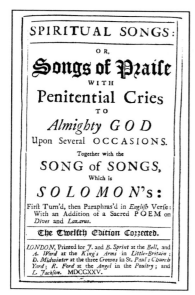

SPIRITUAL SONGS:

OR,

Songs of Praise

WITH

Penitential Cries

TO

Almighty GOD

Upon Several OCCASIONS.

Together with the

SONG of SONGS,

Which is

SOLOMON's:

First Turn'd, then Paraphras'd in *English* Verse:
With an Addition of a Sacred POEM on
Dives and *Lazarus*.

The Twelfth Edition Corrected.

LONDON, Printed for *J.* and *B. Sprint* at the *Bell*, and
A. Ward at the *King's Arms* in *Little-Britain*;
D. Midwinter at the three *Crowns* in St. *Paul's Church*
Yard; *R. Ford* at the *Angel* in the *Poultry*; and
L. Jackson. MDCCXXV.

**Title page of
Thomas Shepard's
*Songs of Praise and
Penitential Cries*, 1725.**

Shepard was a Presbyterian and in his two year ministry in Northampton received £8 per annum from the Presbyterian Fund. He was a considerable theologian and published sermons of note. He was also an accomplished poet and was well-known as the co-author with John Mason of *Penitential Cries*, a series of thirty-two hymns published shortly before his coming to Northampton. In later life he co-operated with Mason in writing *Spiritual Songs* which eclipsed his earlier work; their work certainly paved the way for the hymnody of Isaac Watts and Philip Doddridge. Indeed, one of Shepard's hymns which expresses human pleasure only in knowing Jesus has a close affinity with the great epigram which Doddridge wrote on his family motto which ends with the sentiment, `I live in *pleasure*, when I live to *thee*'.

One very curious event occurred during Shepard's ministry, and one which has long been a puzzle. In the *Church Book* he wrote: `1694. December 11. I married Mr Buswell's Son & Daughter of Kettering in our Meeting House. T. Shepard'. Was this a double wedding? we may ask, and where was the `Meeting House' as work had not started on its construction at that date? The answer to the riddle may be simple; the `Meeting House' was most likely the `Great Meeting' in Kettering (now Toller URC) which had been constructed about 1685, a few years before the Toleration Act. Shepard's father, Revd William Shepard was minister at the Kettering Church from 1695-7 and it is reasonable to suppose that the younger Shepard himself had dealings with this church. Nevertheless, it is curious that he should make such a statement in the Castle Hill *Church Book*, even more so as Dissenting ministers were not allowed by law at that time to perform marriages or bury the dead.

Shepard fell foul of opinion in his church. Perhaps his political views had offended some or were an embarrassment to the church. In accepting his Call he had stressed that pastor and people should walk `comfortably together'. Obviously, matters had become strained with Shepard's heart and mind more spiritually focussed than on the immediate necessities of building and equipping the Meeting House. On 11 September 1696 he wrote in the *Church Book* expressing his disappointment that his flock had forgotten their promises to him:

`At the Church Meeting then holden it was publicly owned by this Church that Thomas Shepard their present Pastor was not under Obligations to a Continuance with them, by virtue of any Obligational Consent or promise made upon sitting down. The Condition not being observ'd by this people, my Engagement to them thereupon must needs cease'.

Shepard left Northampton and after an abortive attempt to aspire to the ministry of the Presbyterian Church assembling in Poor Jewry lane, Aldgate in London he settled at Bocking-cum-Braintree in Essex. Here he found a different and more receptive congregation to whom he ministered with great success for almost forty years. He died in 1739.

**The puzzling Buswell wedding entry in the
*Church Book***

Revd John Hunt: 1698 - 1709

Throughout 1697 the Castle Hill Church, although pastorless, was not without leadership. On 5 February it was decided to call a Church Meeting every month on the Friday before each Lord's Day. On 3 September the diaconate was strengthened by the appointment of John Rigby ` to execute the Office of Deacon & he manifesting his Acceptance of that Call was accordingly on that day enstated and empowered by the Churches Act'. On 25 February 1698 `the Church did then consent to call Mr John Hunt to be their Pastor which call he embraced and at that time entered upon the Pastoral charge'.

Hunt's father had been ejected from his living at Sutton in Cambridgeshire. Hunt came to Northampton from Royston and it is said that he suited the people better than Shepard. A talented man, well versed in the Scriptures and zealous in his advocacy of truth he brought a powerful personality to his ministry. He was the right man at the right time well able to steer the church through the dangerous waters of theological controversy which characterises the turn of the century. Hunt was determined to uphold truth with ruggedness and firmness. Writing of himself in one of his published works, *The Infants' Faith*, he justified his style of ministry:

`...for since God hath set me a watchman over this flock I think myself bound - as ever I hope to give up my account with joy - to take all the care of them I can, and do my utmost to reduce such as are wandering, and establish such as are wavering; and to keep the plague out of their head as well as their hands from being defiled; judging a blind eye rather than a lame foot.   Errors in judgement are like to be an inlet into continual errors in practice'.*

Hunt's iron-rod rule is reflected in the *Church Book* which notes on 28 September 1699 that `It was agreed upon by this Society that it should be left to Mr Hunt our Pastor to determine whom it shall be lawful for us to hear preach and it shall be judged an offence to the Church to act in that case contrary to his determination'. Hunt clearly wanted to eradicate the preaching of error in his church thus minimising controversy.

Nevertheless the issue of Baptism became vexatious with some six members of Castle Hill transferring allegiance to College Lane. Names in the *Church Book* are crossed out with heavy ink lines with comments such as `rent offe to Mr More' (i.e. the Baptist minister at College Lane). Although Hunt's writings excited controversy he succeeded in the main in minimising the effects of `disorders' on his congregation. As evidence of the church settling down the *Church Book* notes on 1 February 1699: `Agreed on then by the Church that Mr Dust and Mr Sanders should have the use of the Meeting garden for the space of twelve years paying 10 shillings a year. Witness our hands: Wm Burkitt, John Buswell, James Weston, Richard Pendred, George Mason, John Rigby'. There follows a signed declaration by Thomas Dust and John Sanders promising to honour the agreement.

The church under Hunt's ministry grew by some one hundred members. It was a sign of his confident authority that he was instrumental in abolishing the office of Ruling Elder, a vestige of the old Presbyterian rigidity which had itself caused problems in the past. It was a decisive move towards a more Congregational church order in which the Church Meeting became the authority in the church. On 7 May 1707:

`It was agreed upon by the whole Church assembled at a public Church Meeting for weighty reasons for the time to come that the Church shall be governed without ruling Elders. And for preventing all disorders of the Church it was agreed upon nevertheless that no member shall be taken in or put out without the determination of the majority of the Church then present'.

Hunt the strong watchman of his flock had decisively moved the church towards a Congregational future. His ministry was not confined to Castle Hill. Many of the members of the church came from the villages around and he was quick to seize on opportunities to preach the gospel there and establish Dissenting churches in those places. His ministry in Northampton closed in 1709 after eleven years intense work. He moved to Newport Pagnell in an exchange of charges with the Revd Thomas Tingey. While in Newport Pagnell he published a volume of *Hymns and Spiritual Songs* which are characterised by an earnest sincerity. He later moved to Tunstead in Norfolk where he continued his literary and ministerial activities until his death, probably in 1730.

Revd Thomas Tingey: 1709 - 1729

Thomas Tingey trained for the ministry under the Revd Thomas Goodwin of Pinner, Middlesex. Tingey started his ministry at Newport Pagnell and after ten years interchanged with John Hunt to take over the pastorate at Castle Hill. The *Church Book* records:

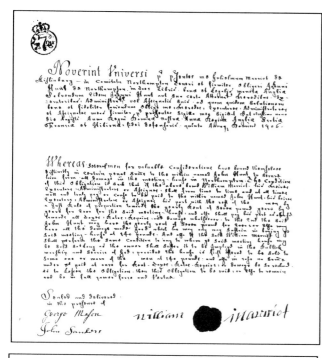

Early deed securing the trusteeship of the Meeting House and the payment of the minister (Rev John Hunt) of £7 rent per annum.

Memorial to Rev John Hunt and his family at Castle Hill.

'This Church having before invited & called the Revd. Mr. Tho: Tingey to take upon him the pastoral care of their souls & and after the removal of the Reverend Mr John Hunt brought the said Revd. Mr. Tho: Tingey & his family to Northampton, did after diverse repeated Calls & days & times of seeking God, the day above-written, solemnly & unanimously renew their Call at which time the said Revd. Mr. Tho: Tingey gave his acceptance thereof, together with the reasons of it, & was solemnly ordained unto ye pastoral office & charge of the Church of Christ'.

Tingey commenced a ministry of considerable consolidation. Under his care the church 'prospered in numbers, piety and zeal'. The *Church Book* records page after page of the names of newly admitted members in Tingey's handwriting; there are some 210 names. Upon coming into membership new members heard the church covenant read out before being received; one such person in 1710 'spake his experience viva voce to the satisfaction of the church and was received by way of covenant and by prayer'. Unlike his predecessors Tingey was not given to controversy and chose to conduct his ministry with a warm and sympathetic earnestness. He poured his energies into his work and preached much in Northampton and in the villages around. The Church Book attested to his wide influence as members were admitted from a considerable radius of the town.

The 'gathered' nature of the church is witnessed in the early deeds relating to the Meeting House. The first men who purchased the Castle Hill site were the actual freeholders of the property. Carefully they took advantage of their civil rights to ensure that the property was set aside in perpetuity as a place of worship. In 1703 an indenture was drawn up ensuring this. By 1711 another indenture named nineteen trustees. During John Hunt's ministry other legal moves enabled him as minister to be part of the ownership of the church and receive financial considerations; thus an early provision for some remuneration for his labours had been made. This 1711 indenture transferred the same rights that Hunt enjoyed to Tingey, one being that if any part of the premises was sold off the minister should be paid its value. It was an attempt to give some security to the ministry.

1711, of course, was the year of the *Occasional Conformity Act* which was aimed at increasing persecution of Dissenters. With the reign of Queen Anne a period of reaction had set in and, had she dared, the Queen would have destroyed the political and social influence of all Dissenters. The act levied fines of £40 on anyone holding civil or military office if found frequenting a place of worship other than the Established Church. Of more sinister design was the *Schism Act* of 1714 which aimed at preventing anyone from keeping any public or private school or teaching in any capacity who were not communicant members of the Established Church. The act struck hard at the roots of Nonconformist strength, their academies, and was to become a major issue for Philip Doddridge twenty years later. The 1711 indenture reflects the restrictive legislation; the trustees of the church are ineligible to act unless they live within six miles of the property. For a 'consideration' of 'one hundred and forty pounds of good lawful money of Great Britain' they had fully discharged Hunt's legal title to the property. Tingey's wife Ann is a signatory to the document showing how she and her husband's livelihood were bound up in its provisions. It is interesting to note the names, occupations and habitations of the trustees at that time:

'Reverend Thomas Tingey, clerk; James Hackleton, bodice maker; George Mason, milliner; Peter Dunkley, wheelwright; Edward Dunkley' wheelwright; Miles Burkitt, hosier; Richard Pendred, currier; Thomas Dust, haberdasher of hats; William Bliss, chandler; Josian Bryne, collarmaker all of the said town of Northampton...Thomas Teton of Denton...gent; Thomas Roe of Great Houghton...yeoman; Francis Langford of Wootton...yeoman; Richard Folwell of Eastcourt...gent; Thomas Manning of Kislingbury...comber; Richard Ward of Nether Heyford...yeoman; Thomas Hipwell of Upper Heyford...yeoman; Richard Stanton of Kingsthorpe...yeoman; and Samuel Stanton of Dallington...yeoman'.

Following the death of Queen Anne in 1714 the *Occasional Conformity Act* and the *Schism Act* were repealed (1718/1719 respectively) and Dissenters began to breathe a sigh of relief. Tingey took the opportunity to ensure the certification of the Meeting House. On 15 July 1718 J. Horton, Clerk to the Justices of the peace, signed and sealed the following document:

14

'These are to certify that Thomas Tingey Clerk did certify to His Majesty's Justices of the Peace assembled at the General Quarter Sessions of the Peace held for the County of Northampton on Tuesday the fifteenth day of July anno domini 1718 that all that New erected building of the said Thomas Tingey with the appurtenances situated being and near adjoining unto Castle Hill in the parish of St Peter's in the Town of Northampton in the said County of Northampton is set apart and intended a place of Meeting for Protestant Dissenters to meet for the purpose of their religious worship and praise of God given under my hand and the Law of my Office this fifteenth day of July Anno Domini 1718'.

Of necessity the construction of the Meeting House in 1695 had to be a hurried affair, and recently discovered indentures dated 1739 and 1751 point to a fact hitherto not known:

'the said trustees since the said purchase of the said premises have pulled down the said building lately used as a Meeting house or place of Religious worship and have upon the ground on which the same stood and upon other part of the aforesaid toft, plot, piece or parcel of Ground erected and built another Building which is now likewise used as a Meeting house or place of Religious worship'.

`The Certificate for ye New Building July 15th 1718'

The first building was soon improved upon and enlarged in the early years of its existence. This might explain the odd fact that the 1695 datestone is not built into the walls of the church, (although it has been generally supposed that it was removed from the North wall when extensions were made in 1862). Solid documentary evidence, however, points to the fact that the Meeting House was rebuilt, hence the need for Tingey to register it in 1718. The certificate (quoted above) is entitled `The Certificate for ye New Building' and dated 15 July 1718. Indentures dated before 1718 refer to the Meeting House as being `latterly erected' but this specifically refers to `that New erected building of the said Thomas Tingey'. Subsequent indentures (as above) speak of `another Building'. It is therefore clear that the Meeting House was rebuilt some twenty-three years after its initial foundation, at a time when persecution of Dissenters was easing. It was another moment when opportunity had to be grasped.

This tabernacle in the wilderness was characterised by great simplicity; a square barn of a place with heavily shuttered windows that were made necessary by the occasional mobs who would hurl dung and stones during services of worship. The dimensions of the enlarged Meeting House were 39ft 4ins (12m) north to south, and 52ft 6ins (16m) east to west. A small vestry was constructed at the intersection of the north and west walls, and the pulpit was placed against the north wall and reached by ten steps. One description of the interior states:

'Space for about seven hundred persons. Roof propped up by two great white wooden pillars, one a little bandy - the `Jachin' and `Boaz' of the temple. White galleries, clumsy white pulpit, a great sounding board over it. Right and left of it, glazed with small, gray-green panes, two small windows of the lattice kind.

Straight before the pulpit, a long massive communion table; and over this table, on a chain that dangled from the rafters, a mighty brass branched candlestick. All the pews near the walls were deep and square. There were no lobbies. You went up the gallery steps in the sight of all Israel; and the doors opened right into the graveyard, grassy, still and peaceful. Within and without everything was marked by stark plainness'. (PDN Ch 3 note 29).

At the commencement of Tingey's ministry the differences between College Lane and Castle Hill became acute. The invitation by the deacons of Castle Hill to College Lane to send `their Elder & Messengers to behold...the solemn occasion of Mr Tingey's being set apart for the pastoral office' had been turned down. A month later College Lane enquired how far Castle Hill allowed ministers of the Church of England to preach in the Meeting House, whether it was in communion with the Presbyterians or how strictly the church dealt with `offenders' to its rules. A cool relationship developed from 1710 but the action of a certain Mrs Davis, a member of the Rothwell Church who also worshipped at College Lane brought matters to a head; she expressed a desire `to sit down with Mr Tingey's people as well'. College Lane refused her request. It was something of a test case. Even the strict Rothwell Church who had expressed disapproval of Castle Hill in the past, forbidding a Mrs Hardin from receiving communion there until it was ascertained that the church was `a true Church of Christ', seemed more conciliatory. On 30 March 1712 the Rothwell Church considered `Sister' Davis' request and testified that `in the first founding of Mr Tingey's church, and in their after and present proceedings, it is chiefly Congregational'. We do not know the outcome of the matter but, after this, relationships became more cordial; the vestry of Castle Hill was frequently used by the Baptists for the convenience of the minister and candidates for believer's baptism when they were baptised either in a brook that flowed nearby into the River Nene or in the river itself that flowed at the base of the hill. William Carey, the great missionary, was baptised from the Castle Hill vestry on 5 October 1783 at 6am, this early hour being necessary to avoid the abusive attentions of local youth who often frequented the ruined castle walls. The issue of baptism was resolved on a `beg to differ basis' and the two churches have co-operated lovingly and happily ever since. In 1981 the United Reformed Church brought both forms of baptism within its scope.

Tingey's ministry was an essential preparation ground for the future, a vital interlinking of the ministries of Blower, Shepard and Hunt with that of Doddridge. Tingey's energetic efforts undermined his health and he resigned the pastorate towards the close of 1728. He moved to the popular Meeting House in Fetter Lane, London and was ordained to his new charge on 5 March 1729. Unfortunately he died on 1 November of the same year, enfeebled by his exertions. His body is buried in the Dissenting burial ground at Bunhill Fields.

Part 3
The ministry of
the Revd Philip Doddridge
1729 - 1751

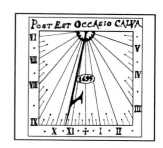

The Man

Philip Doddridge's arrival in Northampton on Christmas Eve 1729 began a new chapter in the history of Castle Hill. Since Tingey's removal the church had procured the services of local ministers to conduct worship, and Doddridge came from Market Harborough to preach on several occasions. The church had determined to persuade him to `preach among us a month as a Candidate in order for whole Satisfaction'. After initial hesitation Doddridge accepted the Call. His stipend from the church was to be about £70 per annum although this was to be supplemented by £20 a year from London and £30 from his Academy `pupils' who were transferring with him. He set up house at the corner of Marefair and Pike Lane; although the Castle Hill folk gave him £50 worth of furniture he had to borrow £100 in order to convert his house to accommodate the expected students.

Philip Doddridge learning Bible stories at his mother's knee.

The move to Northampton was the culmination of a long and arduous pilgrimage. Born in 1702 somewhere in London Philip Doddridge was the twentieth child born to his mother; eighteen of his brothers and sisters had either been stillborn or had died in infancy. He had one living sister, Elizabeth. Initially considered to be stillborn Doddridge did survive. Named after an uncle he never enjoyed robust health and was always frail and consumptive. His family background was steeped in Dissent, his maternal grandfather having escaped from religious persecution in Bohemia and his paternal grandfather having been one of the ejected two thousand in 1662. Doddridge's mother died when he was only eight years old and his father when he was just thirteen. Yet they had lavished their care on their children, Doddridge recalling that his mother had taught him the history of the Old and New Testaments by the aid of the Dutch tiles in the fireplace before he could read.

After a guardian squandered the inheritance that Doddridge had been left he was befriended by Revd Samuel Clark, a Presbyterian minister in St Albans. Clark ensured that Doddridge entered into the Dissenting Academy at Kibworth in Leicestershire. Founded in 1715 and conducted by the Revd John Jennings the Academy had a high reputation. Doddridge commenced in the autumn of 1719 and spent three years in study, removing with the Academy to Hinckley and qualifying as a Christian minister in 1723 and being ordained to the pastorate at Kibworth. However, the premature death of Jennings in that year resulted in Doddridge being persuaded to take over the principalship of the Academy. Having agreed to the task his announcement that he was removing to Northampton caused him and his Market Harborough friends much anguish. His arrival in Northampton, therefore, had much emotion attached to it and, as he set about his new ministry Doddridge was conscious of new beginnings. Within a year he had met, wooed and married Mercy Maris, like himself an orphan, whom he had met in Worcester. Their marriage was a superb relationship and they had nine children, five of whom died in infancy.

Their first child, Elizabeth (nicknamed Tetsy) died a week before her fifth birthday of consumption; she is buried in the Castle Hill Church.

The Minister

Doddridge's ministry at Castle Hill was ambitious in its scope and remarkable in its effectiveness. He was formally `ordained a Presbyter' by eight ministers who gathered with the congregation to `solemnly set him apart to the Office of the Ministry and the Pastoral Care of the Church of Northampton by the Laying on of Hands, with Fasting and Prayer, at the Town of Northampton aforesaid, on the Nineteenth day of March 1729-30'.

Doddridge had a clear, loud voice and preached with a `nervous violence' and `earnest tenderness'. The Meeting House was usually filled with a cross-section of society: shopkeepers and tradesmen, farmers, farm workers and local villagers, soldiers stationed temporarily in the town, local gentry and intelligentsia. On the Lord's Day crowded services were held both morning and afternoon. Before the afternoon service Doddridge catechised the children. Usually no evening service was held except once a month when the Lord's Supper was celebrated. This service was of immense importance to Doddridge. Lunar phases dictated when this was held as a full Moon diminished the hazardous nature of the waggon tracks which served as roads for those who came from the countryside. The fear of robbery was also another concern. Doddridge and his students would give special lectures on Sunday evenings from time to time.

The Revd Philip Doddridge D.D

When Doddridge commenced his ministry congregational hymn singing was in its infancy. Before *the Toleration Act* Dissenters had little desire to advertise their presence by singing, and such singing, especially by women, was considered by some to be carnal and worldly. The pioneering work of Doddridge's great friend, Isaac Watts, in composing hymns resulted in the growing popularity of hymn singing. Doddridge began to compose his own, illustrating the points of his sermons which were usually the social implications of the Gospel. Altogether his published hymns amount to 375 and have appeared in most major denominational hymnals . Somewhat tone deaf and lacking an organ or choir Doddridge relied on his clerk to lead the singing using the technique of `lining out' i.e. repeating each line or couplet.

Doddridge had an extraordinary gift in prayer which he was diligent to develop. He would spend many hours in the vestry reviewing in prayer his own spiritual state and the welfare of the congregation and his students. He was concerned that he did not visit his people as often as he would like, and had an especial interest in children and young people. He encouraged religious associations amongst the young people of the congregation and distributed religious literature to them.

In order to cope with the heavy pastoral load Doddridge restored the office of elder, formally dispensed with by Hunt in 1707. Accordingly on 26 Feb 1741 the *Church Book* records the appointment of four elders to assist him and the six deacons. Doddridge wrote a set of *Counsels* to his elders, advising them how to approach their duties using commonsense, diplomacy and compassion. Discipline within the church he considered important and regarding cases of public scandal he considered that offenders be publically admonished if private admonition had failed. On 16 April 1741 seven cases causing scandal were brought before the church meeting; three men were censured for drunkenness and one for profane speech. Families that had quarrelled were reconciled and one man who frequented alehouses thus neglecting his family and trade was 'exhorted to Repentance, Humiliation and Reformation'. Others who by their own fault had become bankrupt, thereby causing distress to creditors were censured and excommunicated. Doddridge, nevertheless, found such necessary actions distressing.

The Northampton Academy in Sheep Street, 1751.

The Teacher

Doddridge's Academy immediately became successful. His house at No 34 Marefair was not large enough to accommodate all the students who wished to come. In 1740 he and Mercy moved to the Earl of Halifax's town house in Sheep Street, a prominent position in the town. The rental was fixed at £40 per annum and a number of servants were necessary in its administration. In its twenty-two years of existence some two hundred students were educated at the Northampton Academy. It was an open institution with no tests of religious belief exacted upon the students. Some were educated in order to enter the Anglican ministry, others came in preference to the universities of Oxford and Cambridge whose academic level at that time was low. Students originated from every region of the country as well as from Holland and Scotland. Although the majority trained for the Nonconformist ministry others entered a variety of trades and professions.

Students had to rise from their beds at six o'clock in the summer and seven in the winter. Doddridge was always up early, rising at five and ready for them when they assembled for morning prayers. Every morning at eight family prayers were said when a chapter from the Old Testament was read in Hebrew by a senior student; Doddridge then expounded upon the text. Every evening a chapter from the New Testament was similarly read in Greek and expounded upon. Breakfast followed family prayers and students could choose to eat 'with the Tutor in his Parlour or at the other Tea Board in the great Parlour'. Students were forbidden to hang around the kitchens, were fined if they gave essays in late, failed to return library books, were late at prayers and lectures or failed to perform allotted duties or came in late at night after the gates were locked. They were forbidden to frequent the local ale houses 'on penalty of a publick Censure for the first Time, & the Forfeiture of a shilling the second'. A degree of democracy was exercised in the organisation of the Academy and the students had opportunity to voice their concerns. There was a strong bond of affection between Doddridge and the students, particularly as they shared in the deaths of several students through illness and accident. Occasionally Doddridge made the difficult decision to expel a student for continual ill-discipline.

Doddridge divided his students into classes and usually lectured to them every morning except Thursdays. He set them much course work and research linked with his lectures and insisted that by the end of their first year all students should master his system of shorthand which he had used since the age of fourteen. Most students had to learn Latin and Greek. Hebrew was taught as was French, history, anatomy, mathematical & scientific subjects, divinity, ethics and 'pneumatology' (psychology); indeed, Doddridge was a pioneer in teaching this last subject and also the first to lecture in English rather than the traditional Latin. Part of the theological students' course was to have preaching experience. To this end the students would sit in the table pew at Castle Hill and take down Doddridge's sermons which they were then expected to preach as 'repetitions'. On one occasion on 21 October 1736 one of his students was about to lead a service of worship in a cottage in Brixworth when an anti-Dissenting mob stormed the house, smashing windows and threatening the student's life. He promptly escaped by climbing out of a back window. The owner of the cottage was almost drowned by the mob in the horse pond. Outraged by the incident Doddridge, in spite of the reluctance of the local justice of the peace, saw justice done and compensation awarded for the damage.

Experience had made Doddridge wary that the civil rights of Dissenters were far from satisfactory. In 1732 he had been criticised by the Rector of Kingsthorpe for his preaching in a barn in that village. Following this the Consistory Court of All Saints summoned him to appear to answer to him not being licenced by the Established Church to teach young people; he was to be questioned as to his 'Learning and Dexterity in teaching' and his 'right understanding of God's true religion' and his 'honest and sober Conversation'. At stake was more than Doddridge's fitness to teach; it was an issue that affected all Dissenters. A mob attacked his house in Marefair, stoning the windows. Doddridge sought wider support and the matter became of national interest. Eventually the king, George II intervened declaring 'that in his reign there should be no persecutions for conscience sake'. A significant advance in equality in education had been made for every Dissenter, the whole issue of Nonconformist liberties being debated in parliament in June 1734.

The Northampton Academy received widespread publicity and Doddridge was asked to furnish the *Constitutions Orders & Rules* relating to the academy to the new universities across the Atlantic: Yale College, Connecticut and New Jersey (now Princeton University). Doddridge was greatly respected within the universities of Oxford and Cambridge, and a singular honour was awarded him in 1736 by Aberdeen University in the conferring of an honorary Doctorate of Divinity. All his students gathered to congratulate their beloved tutor on his award. Upon Doddridge's death in 1751 the academy moved to Daventry under Dr Caleb Ashworth but returned to Northampton in 1789 under the then minister of Castle Hill, the Revd John Horsey. It continued in various forms until 1977 as a school of divinity within the University of London.

Doddridge's concern in education was not confined to his academy. In 1738 his congregation supported him in establishing a charity school in which twenty boys were put under the skilful care of John Browne of Castle Hill as their teacher. The boys were provided with clothes and were brought to church. Student fines in the Academy were used to support the school the location of which is not known. Doddridge hoped to add girls to the school but there is no record of this being accomplished. The school closed, possibly in 1772, but it influenced the foundation of similar institutions in Leicester, Hinckley and elsewhere.

The Author

Doddridge's deep desire to see a well-educated ministry stemmed from a deeply-held concern for Christian truth; error needed to be combatted by sound understanding. Thus at every opportunity, and often at his own expense, he published sermons, pamphlets and books. The effort which went into his literary output was immense. Rising early every morning he put in several hours' work before breakfast. He grasped every precious moment of his life having since his childhood regarded 'the best recreation is in the change from one work to another'. His published works are numerous, many being several volumes in extent. *The Rise and Progress of Religion in the Soul* (1745) was acclaimed the best book of the eighteenth century and is a lasting monument to Doddridge's genius. Translated into numerous languages it touched many lives influencing William Wilberforce, acclaimed by the Princess of Wales and changing the life Dr James Stonhouse who became Doddridge's partner in the foundation of the Northampton Infirmary. Another great work was *The Family Expositor* which took Doddridge twelve years of intense effort. He did not live to see the sixth and final volume published in 1756. The first edition quickly sold out and it was reprinted many times, retaining its popularity for over a century. His translation of the New Testament from the original Greek including commentaries and devotional exercises was the first work of its kind aimed at giving the public an opportunity of studying the scriptures with open and alert minds. William Carey took a copy with him to India and used it when translating the New Testament into Bengali. It had a profound effect on popular understanding of heaven as the *home* for the exiled human spirit.

Doddridge was convinced that the family held the key to religious education and accordingly aimed much of his literary output to this cause: *Sermons on the...Education of children, Sermons to Young Persons* and *A plain and serious address to the Master of a Family on the Important Subject of family-religion* are but a few of his works. *The Principles of the Christian religion...in...verse...for the use of little Children* (1743) was even used by the royal family, the future George III learning the verses by heart. Together with Isaac Watts Doddridge 'opened up a range of thought and feeling far beyond the conception of their Protestant forbears'. (PDN143).

The Man of Social Conscience

The population of Northampton in Doddridge's time ranged between four and five thousand; there were as many horses in the town as people. It was a busy place, and the Castle Hill Church and the Academy had become well-known landmarks. Doddridge busied himself in the town's life, trying without success to save the lives of two men condemned to death for murder. He was concerned with the events of his time: cattle disease, the great earthquake of 1750, scientific investigations and the ever-present threat of early death (especially in children) from smallpox and tuberculosis.

When smallpox was raging in local villages Doddridge published a pamphlet written twenty-five years earlier by David Some on the importance of inoculation against the disease. This publication was widely read and paved the way for a change of attitude on the part of the public towards inoculation which hitherto was considered contrary to divine will. Doddridge well knew the tragedy of losing family and friends through disease and determined to do something practical for the general health of the town. Together with Stonhouse he campaigned and organised the town's first Infirmary which opened formally on 29 March 1744 in a hastily adapted house in George Row. The venture was a success from its inception and for the rest of his life Doddridge supported it in financial and many practical ways.

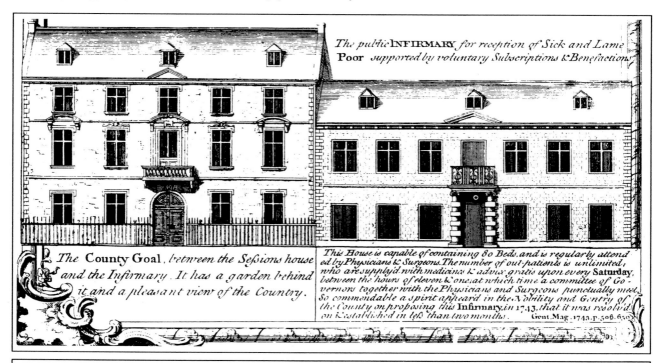

The County Goal, between the Sessions house and the Infirmary. It has a garden behind it and a pleasant view of the Country.

The public INFIRMARY for reception of Sick and Lame Poor supported by voluntary Subscriptions & Benefactions

This House is capable of containing 80 Beds, and is regularly attended by Physicians & Surgeons. The number of out-patients is unlimited, who are supply'd with medicine & advice gratis upon every Saturday, between the hours of eleven & one; at which time a committee of Governors together with the Physicians and Surgeons punctually meet. So commendable a spirit appeard in the Nobility and Gentry of the County on proposing this Infirmary, in 1743, that it was resolvd on & established in less than two months. Gent. Mag. 1743. p. 506. 650

The County Gaol and Infirmary, George Row, Northampton. Doddridge sought to save felons from the gallows at the rear of the gaol, and started Northampton's first infirmary in 1744.

Like all Dissenters Doddridge was an ardent supporter of the Hanoverian monarchy simply because they were eminently preferable to the Stuarts. Political instability edied constantly in the background and Doddridge feared, as did other perceptive Dissenters, that persecution might well return. The summer of 1745 confirmed his worst fears when Charles Edward Stuart, the Young Pretender, landed in the Hebrides, raised his standard at Glenfinnan and claimed the throne of England on behalf of his father. One of Doddridge's most ardent members of the congregation, Colonel James Gardiner, was killed by the Jacobites at the Battle of Prestonpans. Doddridge was galvanised into action. Supported by leading figures at Castle Hill, other ministers and congregations, local gentry (especially the Earl of Halifax who lived at Horton) a force of 814 men was raised in Northampton ready to repel invasion; the Duke of Bedford recruited a similar number and the Duke of Montagu provided 273 cavalry. Northampton became a centre of military activity. On 5 November 1745 the church bells rang, civic leaders attended All Saints Church and drank loyal toasts to the King at the Guildhall. That night a great bonfire was lit outside the Academy with fireworks, and candles that spelt out the defiant message 'King George, No Pretender'. Later that month the town was in panic as news reached them that the Jacobites had reached Derby. Battle was contemplated on Harlestone Heath, but the Young Pretender, disappointed by the lack of support to his cause and knowledgeable of the warm reception awaiting him at Northampton, turned back for Scotland. Doddridge had been the first civilian in the entire country to take action in the defence of the realm.

Throughout his twenty-one years in Northampton Doddridge had tried to fulfil an active social involvement. He sought to engender in his congregation a wider vision which took the church forward into a deeper engagement with society around it. Doddridge's activities in the Academy, his writing and voluminous correspondence which resulted in his position as one of the foremost leaders of Dissent meant that he had limited time for the minutiae of life at Castle Hill. He confessed that his life was like a hare being chased by the hounds at its heels and tried hard to fit in his visitations to the families and the sick. Doddridge made great efforts at delegation relying on his elders and deacons in covering much pastoral responsibility. Towards the close of his ministry it became apparent to him that numerically the church was in a state of decline. At Michaelmas 1745 he drew up a list of church members; of those surviving and remaining from the time of his ordination and induction in March 1730 sixty-six remained plus 234 whom he had admitted as members. The inroads of the Moravians on Castle Hill became of serious concern to him. At one time he had been impressed by Moravian missionary effort and evangelism, but when on 1 June 1749 six members, including an elder, withdrew to the Moravian Church he became even more worried. He commented with feeling in the *Church Book*: 'Rent off to the Moravians; not to be readmitted till they are convinced of their error'. He concluded that membership had fallen from 300 at Michaelmas 1745 to 239 in December 1749, a drop of 61 in just over four years.

Somehow matters seemed to be slipping from his control as Doddridge's exertions eventually took a heavy toll on his health. Prepared for death at any time he always expressed his thankfulness each birthday for having lived another year. By the early part of 1751 he was on the verge of a complete breakdown; by June he admitted that he looked much older and his hoarse cough was getting no better. He had all the symptoms of consumption. Accompanied by Mercy he travelled by carriage to the hot wells in Bristol hoping for some relief; but this, together with the tar water and asses milk prescribed by his physicians, did little good. Further advice to travel to a warmer, drier climate in Lisbon was also taken but proved fatal when the rainy season set in. Doddridge died on 26 October 1751 and is buried in the Protestant cemetery attached to the British Factory in Lisbon where his grave and tomb may still be visited. The Castle Hill *Church Book* simply records:

'The Revd. P. Doddridge, D.D., after being Twenty One Years Pastor of this Church died at Lisbon (to which Place he resorted for the Recovery of his Health) on the 26th of October 1751. We may truly say to the Unspeakable Loss of this Church'.

Doddridge's ministry was of immense significance far wider than Castle Hill or Northampton. His universal appeal was summarised by Bishop Jebb who paid tribute to him as 'a burning and shining light which, in days of more than ordinary coldness, Divine Providence was pleased to enkindle, in order to impart both warmth and illumination to the professing Christian world'. (PDN143)

CASTLE·HILL

Dr Doddridge's Vestry

Drawn by W.J.Rush.

Part 4
1751 - 1859
The ministries of Gilbert, Hextal, Horsey, Hyatt and Bennett.

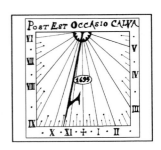

Revd Robert Gilbert: 1753 - 1760

Doddridge had hoped (and had specified in his will) that his faithful assistant, the Revd Job Orton, should replace him both as principal of the academy and minister at Castle Hill. Orton's removal to Shrewsbury in 1741 dashed such a prospect. In 1749, as an alternative, Doddridge specified his wish that the Revd Caleb Ashworth should be his successor. However, Ashworth, who was assistant minister at the Independent Church in Daventry, whilst willing to take over the responsibility for the Academy, felt himself unable to move to Northampton. His co-pastor, the Revd James Floyd, had left Daventry leaving Ashworth in sole charge. The Castle Hill Church prudently realised that to find someone of the stature of Doddridge was going to be a difficult if not impossible task. Attempts were made to enlist the services of two of Doddridge's ministerial friends: Dr John Guyse of New Bond Street, London, and Dr David Jennings, formerly of Kibworth, but currently a professor at the Hoxton Academy. Both ventures came to naught and it was a year before a new minister was inducted to the pastorate. In the meantime, for six months, Castle Hill generously paid Doddridge's salary to his bereaved family, and students from the Academy continued the preaching ministry of the church.

The task of following a man of such stature as Doddridge was a daunting prospect. 'The mourning church did not readily find a pastor to take the place of the pious Doctor Doddridge, whose good qualities were ever present to the members now that he was no more'(TG37). Even experienced ministers and students were loth to follow such a famous preacher. At one church meeting a young man who had been a student at the Academy shouted out that they might as well send for the Pope; at this an uproar ensued resulting in the breaking-up of the meeting. The *Church Book* records laconically that 'The Revd. Mr. Robt. Gilbert of Oakham, was called to be the Pastor of this Church, which Call he accepted of & entered upon the Pastoral Charge on Lady Day 1753'.

Gilbert found the church at Castle Hill in an altered frame of mind since the death of Doddridge, the removal of his wife Mercy and the family to Tewkesbury that year, and the departure of the Academy to Daventry. The memories of his illustrious predecessor were constant and everywhere. Gilbert was assisted in his ministry by William Warburton, the latter preaching in the mornings and Gilbert preaching in the evenings and administering the Lord's Supper. Warburton was appointed as pastor of the Congregational Church at Creaton after Gilbert death in 1760, although he had preached at Creaton every afternoon for the past seven years. The quiet joint ministry of Gilbert and Warburton continued. Although a Master of Arts Gilbert refused to use any titles of distinction, even 'Reverend', wanting to be simply known as 'Robert Gilbert'. This in itself was a stark contrast to the adulation of his predecessor *Doctor Doddridge*.

In 1755 a massive earthquake destroyed much of Lisbon with huge loss of life. Naturally such news caused great concern, not the least for the fact that the earthly remains of Philip Doddridge were placed there. Only three of Gilbert's sermons were published, and in one preached on 6 February 1756 he used his congregation's awareness of the Lisbon situation and the Doddridge connection to good effect:

'Poor creatures! at this distance, it chills my blood to think of their agonising distress, when their fears urged them to fly and yet would not suffer them to advance...Many stood still and perished. Others ran they

knew not wither, as long as they could keep their feet on a pavement that tottered under them. Many died of the fright. Some hundreds trampled under foot were suffocated, and in their delirium many took to the sea and perished... And it must have been very affecting to have seen their Sovereign...sadly complaining though a king of wanting subjects...without a habitation, without money, without bread. A loud and alarming voice from heaven proclaiming that princes and peasants are equally dependent upon the chief and only Potentate, proclaiming the vanity of human affluence and grandeur, and the instability of all earthly possessions'.

Gilbert, like most Dissenters, was exceedingly loyal to the Hanoverian monarchy and supported George II when he called for national days of 'general and public fasting, humiliation and prayer'. In his published sermons 'we can see the man with a fertile mind, a sober judgment, an eloquent tongue, and a tender heart'(AC149). Such tenderness is seen in his attitude towards the natural world. With cattle plague destroying many local herds Gilbert turned his hearers attention to the God-given reality of the natural world:

'...it will greatly increase our sensibility and concern, if we reflect upon the value and usefulness of these creatures which by the wise ordination of a benevolent providence were placed among us to increase our riches, and contribute to our comfort and happiness...But alas! we have been setting ourselves up as the lords of his creation, and have forgotten God to whom we are indebted for such useful creatures, and for all the comforts and conveniences we have enjoyed by their means'.

Like his predecessor Gilbert wrote hymns to illustrate the themes of his sermons many of which hit hard at the hypocrisy of the human heart: 'Instead of censuring the vices of others...everyone should scrutinise himself', he declared on one occasion. No doubt he had cause to speak plainly as some had left the church, attracted by the preaching of Revd John Ryland at College Lane. Others had removed to 'the Meeting on the Green'. Having removed themselves, however, they continued to cause problems by interfering in Castle Hill's affairs. The Church Book records on 5 June 1760:

'Resolved, that after this day, it shall be deemed irregular & absurd, for Such Persons, as have chose to Separate themselves from our Communion (without removing to a Distance, where they probably may not be known) to apply to us for their Dismission - or for any Such Persons, as have adjoin'd themselves to any other Congregation, to interpose in any Consultation, Debate or publick Act whatsoever, relating to the Affairs of this Society, of which, by their voluntary Separation, they declare themselves to be no longer members'.

The social composition of the church had changed, and this is evidenced by the Northamptonshire Subscription List which was drawn up in 1757 as a 5% loan 'to defray the Expenses of the War with France'. Loans of £100 and over were given, and it is significant that over a half of the loans came from members of Castle Hill or its congregation. This wealth and social influence 'were soon to prove the cause of its greatest trouble...already the blighting effects were being felt of having among the worshippers men who considered that their money alone raised them above their fellows, and membership continued slowly to decrease. Mr. Gilbert died before the cloud broke' (TG38).

Gilbert died on Sunday 28 December 1760 whilst sitting in his chair at home in the same placid manner as he had lived. He was 52 years of age and left a widow and two daughters. The *Northampton Mercury* reported his death: 'an eminent Dissenting minister in this Town; remarkable for his Learning, Modesty, Evenness of Temper, and universal Charity; whose loss can only be known by Those, who, among his other Virtues, had opportunities of observing his Conjugal and Parental Tenderness'. He was buried the following Thursday night at a crowded service conducted by Revd Caleb Ashworth.

Revd William Hextal: 1762 - 1775

Revd William Hextal

Eighteen months passed between the death of the 'worthy' Mr Gilbert and the introduction of his successor. Membership of the church continued its decline and preachers 'supplied the pulpit'. Evidently, Caleb Ashworth received the usual fee of a guinea for his preaching but his students only a couple of shillings, apparently for putting up his horse. The only preacher that the church warmed to was the Revd Henry Mayo who came from the Mile End Academy to preach. While the church wavered Mayo accepted a Call from the Nightingale Lane Church, London where he stayed until his death in 1793.

On 18 August 1762 the Rev William Hextal was invited to accept the pastorate. Hextal was a Northamptonshire man, having been born at Broughton near Kettering into a farming family. He had been influenced by the Revd Thomas Saunders of the *Great Meeting* in Kettering and entered the Northampton Academy under Doddridge in 1732. Four years later he became the pastor of the Creaton chapel and was ordained on 26 April 1738 by Philip Doddridge and others 'having given full satisfaction as to his abilities and qualifications for the work of the ministry'. In October of that year his wife Mary gave birth to triplets, a son and two daughters, who were buried three days after they had been baptised. Removing from Creaton in 1751 Hextal became minister of a church in Sudbury, Suffolk where he laboured for ten years until, caught up in the controversies of the political elections of 1761 (when his own plain speaking made it difficult for him to live in peace or work in hope) he responded to the Call to come to Castle Hill.

Hextal's ministry was fraught with disappointment. His early hopes of taking over the Academy proved fruitless. After a few years at Castle Hill theological controversy surrounded him; like Doddridge before him he had allowed George Whitefield to occupy the pulpit at Castle Hill and both men had fallen into trouble because of it. Hextal was accused of Arminianism. Another problem assailed him in the form of a serious and painful medical condition which frequently attacked him without warning. Sometimes the suddenness of these attacks made it impossible to procure a supply from the Daventry Academy. Matters reached a climax in September 1773 when Hextal agreed that the son of Dr J. Winter should preach at Castle Hill for three months with a view to becoming assistant or co-pastor. Young Winter's ministry proved popular and congregations increased. At a church meeting, at which a hundred men were present, it was overwhelmingly resolved to invite Winter to become the 'stated assistant'. But wealthy adherents within the congregation objected strongly to this and intimated their opposition to the decision seeing it as undermining Hextal. Jeremiah Rudsdell, *the Distributor of Stamps for the Counties of Northampton, Warwick and Rutland* and a member of Castle Hill wrote to Winter asking how he expected to be maintained without the support of the principal supporters of the church. Winter's father wrote to Hextal asking him to candidly state his position in the matter. Hextal replied that he had no objections to his son's doctrines and expressed his neutrality as he had 'Friends on both sides'.

However, Hextal was perceived to side with the subscribers and being against young Winter as assistant. This breached the flood gates as the whole question of the nature of the Congregational Church came into question. They charged Hextal with endeavouring *'to subvert the Discipline of the Church being independent, by endeavouring to set aside their Acts. We think it contrary to the temper and spirit of a Christian minister to take those steps and measures which you have taken, by making promises of favour to some, and using threats with others to make them vote according to your pleasure'* He replied to the charges but was dismissed, the victim of a contest largely between members of the church and non-communicants. In spite of a contrary suggestion of asking another person, a Mr Thoroughgood, to become assistant the Church Meeting resolved on 18 April 1775:

'it was this Day agreed by a Majority of Eighteen Brethren of this Church to Dismiss the Revd. Mr Hextal from his Office as Pastor, Minister and Teacher'.

Nineteen members of the church appended their names to the dismissal, `some provision being made for his support'. At first Hextal agreed to resign but then changed his mind. The subscribers then claimed the pulpit and sent formal intimation to the deacons and the chapel keeper that Hextal would be preaching at the usual time the following Sunday, 23 April. The deacons, however, had arranged for a Revd Miller from London to lead the service that day and warned Hextal and his friends not to cause a disturbance. Ten minutes before the usual time of worship Miller went into the pulpit and was introduced to the congregation by a majority of the trustees. Five minutes later Hextal and his supporters arrived and demanded the pulpit. Being informed that he was legally dismissed Hextal gave notice that he would be preaching at the Meeting on the Green that afternoon and hoped his friends would follow him until he recovered his pastoral office by law. The matter continued when Hextal commenced proceedings in the Court of King's Bench but as the church's Trust Deed placed the right of `electing and placing and displacing a minister' in the communicants of the church he abandoned his suit. The *Church Book* has a long entry which reads:

'November 25th 1775, this day came on trial in the Court of King's Bench, in London, between the Rev. Mr. Hextal, who was Plaintiff, and several officers and members of the church, Defendants. A great majority of the church having dismissed him, he applied to the Court for a Rule, to require the defendants to show cause why a Writ of Mandamus should not issue requiring them to restore him to the use of the pulpit of this Meeting. Upon the trial his Counsel endeavoured to overturn the Deed, he and some others making affidavit that former ministers had not been chosen according to the deed, which gives power to the church, upon giving six days public notice by the deacons to elect, place, and displace a minister as they shall think proper. And it is here recorded as a memorable instance of the goodness of God, and a very kind appearance of Providence in our behalf, that the cause was given in our favour; as thereby our properties as men secured to us, which were endeavoured to be taken from us, and our privileges as Christians we had been deprived of had our opponents succeeded, as they were endeavouring to overturn the Independency of the Church, and to bring in subscribers to an equal vote with the Church in the choice of a Minister. May this instance of God's goodness not only be recorded here, but may every member of the Church bear a grateful sense of it continually upon their minds'.

Contention, however, did not end there as disputes continued over the minister's occupation of the church house. Within the possession of the church is a series of documents (wills and indentures) showing the changing ownership of two houses in `the street called Saint Mary's Street in the town of Northampton'. The first document is dated 1665 and the succession continues until 1827. In an indenture dated 21 January 1794 reference is made to another drawn up in 1766 during Hextal's ministry. It refers to the will of a fairly wealthy tradesman, Thomas Holmes, who may have been related to Hextal and who died in the previous year. Holmes left money for the purchase of the two houses with the object of converting them into a single manse for the minister. The 1794 wording states:

'The said Thomas Holmes did in his Life time order and direct his Executors to apply and dispose of one hundred pounds to and for the Use and Benefit of the Minister or pastor for the time being of the Congregation of Protestant Dissenters belonging to the Meeting House near the Hills called the Castle Hills in the said Town of Northampton whereof the said William Hextall was then Minister and Pastor and that the said Executors with the Consent and at the Request of the said William Hextall minded to lay out the said Sum of one hundred pounds in the purchase of the two Messuages or Tenements with the Appurtenances thereinafter mentioned . . . in order that the same premises might be converted into

a Dwelling House for the said William Hextall so long as he should continue Minister or Pastor of the said Congregation and for such other persons who thereafter for the time being should be Ministers or Pastors of the said Congregation to dwell inhabit and reside . . .'.

Memorial to Thomas Holmes at Castle Hill

Holmes also left money for the Charity School which Doddridge had started. The amount of money required for the purchase of the properties exceeded Holmes legacy and a mortgage for £140 was taken out by the twelve trustees ten of whom signed the mortgage deed. When the dispute over possession came to a head it was found on a technicality that the trustees were personally liable for the mortgage money and not the property. The church members insisted on having the house and terms were agreed that Hextal should vacate and that each of the ten trustees (eight of them were of Hextal's party including himself) should pay seven pounds and ten shillings each. In addition the £50 given for the charity school with £5 interest was also handed over to the church.

The dispute rumbled on and differences were aired in the columns of the *Northampton Mercury* and in quarto pamphlets at a shillings each. It was an unseemly dispute in which Thomas Buxton, a deacon of the church, led the church party against Jeremiah Rudsdell who led the Hextal party. Rudsdell's language revealed a contentious un-Christian spirit which classified Hextal's friends as the `principal persons in the congregation' and his opponents as `some paupers, some apprentices, and many labourers and journeymen of different trades...in the lowest situations in life' and indebted to `the principal subscribers...for their daily bread'.

It was clear that a break had to be made. Hextal had continued to preach at the chapel on the Green and took a considerable number of the Castle Hill congregation with him. The *Church Book* gives testimony to the losses suffered by the Castle Hill Church: 21 January 1776 saw eight members cut off because they were `no longer looked upon as standing in a relation to the Church'. Among these was a Mary Doddridge who was certainly not his daughter Mary who had decamped to Tewkesbury with her mother in 1753. On 11 February the haemorage continued with the loss of thirteen others including Jeremiah Rudsdell, Mary Hextal and Mary Wills (whom both Doddridge and Gilbert had encountered because of her oracular powers). Again on 3 March four others left and a week later three more. On 7 April two women were dismissed. On 7 July `At a church meeting held this day Samuel Mellowes Sexton of this Place of Worship and a Member of this Church having previously been reproved for some part of his conduct not being according to the Church was separated from the communion of this church'. On 4 August three others were `dismissed to the Church at College Lane', and there the sad catalogue ends. Those with any sense of humour left might have reflected that whereas Castle Hill had lost thirty-one of its members the Crown had in that same year begun to lose the American War of Independence.

Hextal commenced a new independent church in King's Head Lane, later called King Street. It officially opened on 17 October in the following year, 1777, after intense work on Hextal's part. His first sermon in the new chapel was to be his last for he died on the 4 November aged sixty-six. The chapel was enlarged in 1858 and entirely rebuilt in 1881. It closed in October 1900 `but in the Church assembling at Abington Avenue the continuity of the body of believers who left Castle Hill in 1775 is preserved' (BG45).

Revd John Horsey: 1777 - 1827

Revd John Horsey

Castle Hill Church was left in a greatly weakened state. The officers and members met to survey the damage and reassess the situation. Sixty-five members, a remnant of its past strength, unanimously decided in August 1776 to call the Revd John Horsey to the pastorate. Horsey was the son of a minister of the same name who ministered in Warminster and Ringwood. The younger Horsey had attended Homerton College and had probably supplied for the Castle Hill pulpit after the removal of Hextal. Horsey initially declined the call, being uncertain as to the state of the church after such a traumatic and publicly-known dispute. However, the church renewed the call in the following February and backed up their persistence by sending two of the deacons as emissaries, an unusual occurrence but one not without precedent as messengers had been sent in 1729 to persuade Doddridge to accept the pastoral charge.

Horsey accepted the Call and was received on 13 April 1777 and ordained to his office on 14 May. It was a new beginning with a young minister who had determined to reverse the ravages of the recent past. Congregations improved and some members previously lost with Hextal drifted back. The gathered nature of the church continued with members coming in from many villages around as well as the town. Horsey has been described in these early years thus: `With the grace of God, a cultured mind, polite manners, a genial disposition, the preacher had a fine presence and a handsome face'. He married Hannah the daughter of Revd Samuel King of Welford; he proudly wrote her admission into the *Church Book* on 5 March 1779.

Horsey's ministry was the longest in Castle Hill's entire history being upwards of fifty-one years in length. During this half century much was to happen in the wider world bringing inevitable change to all. Europe was convulsed by the French Revolution in 1789, the Napoleonic Wars and the battles of Trafalgar and Waterloo. The birth of the Sunday School movement in 1783, and a society pledged to the abolition of the Slave Trade four years later signalled a new age of concern for the underprivileged and exploited. The foundation in 1792 in Kettering of the Baptist Missionary Society followed quickly by others, including the London Missionary Society in 1795 and the British and Foreign Bible Society in 1804, opened up the whole challenge of the Gospel to an hitherto undreamed global dimension. Horsey lived to see the repeal of the *Five Mile* and *Conventicle* Acts in 1812 but died one year before the *Test and Corporation Act* was removed from the Statute Book.

Ripples of all these great changes washed into the consciousness of the Castle Hill Church. Horsey had agreed to allow the Revd John Ryland, the younger, of College Lane the use of the vestry for the purpose of preparing a baptism candidate. The name of the twenty-year old candidate was William Carey, the founder of modern missions. Ryland's account of the event reads:

'October 5th, 1783: I baptised in the river Nen, a little beyond Dr. Doddridge's meeting house at Northampton, a poor journeyman shoemaker, little thinking that before nine years had elapsed, he would prove the first instrument of forming a society for sending missionaries from England to preach the gospel to the heathen. Such, however, as the event has proved, was the purpose of the Most High, who selected for this work not the son of one of our most learned ministers, nor one of the most opulent of our dissenting gentlemen, but the son of a parish clerk' (quoted in *The Life of William Carey* by George Smith p12)

1. Castle Hill Chapel
2. "Aunçient Castle Ruynous"
3. The Nene where Carey was baptized.

The location of William Carey's baptism, 17 October 1783 at 6 am.   **William Carey 1761 - 1834**

Horsey was of an amiable, non-dogmatic disposition and the Church book evidences this; on 2 December 1798 the customary practise of admitting members to the church after they had given an oral account or testimony of their spiritual `experience' was dispensed with. Evidently the church meeting had agreed to the decision which was `fairly and peaceably obtained' and it was unanimously passed: `that in conformity to what has been the custom of admitting persons as members of this Church by their delivering in what is called an Experience, any one preferring that mode, shall be at full liberty to adopt it, upon their admission amongst us, but as it is to some an impediment to their obeying the Saviour's dying command, <u>it shall not be insisted upon for the future'</u>. The double underlining is Horsey's.

After Doddridge's death in 1751 the Academy moved to Daventry under the direction of the Revd Caleb Ashworth. The latter's first assistant, Thomas Belsham, had eventually succeeded to the principalship but honorably resigned from his position when his theological convictions clashed with the purpose of his office. Horsey agreed to take over the Academy which duly moved back into Northampton in 1789. Belsham's resignation was the tip of the iceberg of theological controversy which raged in the Academy and in the wider theological sphere. Even Doddridge had been criticised for giving a too open-minded approach to arguments; now Horsey found that the tendency of the age that brought theology into wasteful speculations had infected the Academy. He was unable to arrest the flow of such free-thinking which undermined the Trinitarian basis of Christianity; about half the students who left the Academy were Arian or Unitarian. It was said that Horsey became 'so anxious not to give an undue bias to his pupils, that in the lecture room, it was difficult to ascertain his own views on controverted doctrines'(AC166). Even his three daughters and son became Unitarians. All this, naturally, spread into Castle Hill and Horsey was suspected of being a Unitarian himself. His failure to give a clear and distinct viewpoint on such controversial issues sadly led to a decline in the congregation in his later years; the 169 members admitted during his pastorate less losses by death and removal meant that the church's membership stood at the same level in 1827 as it had in 1777. After nine years struggling with both duties of Church and Academy Horsey decided to resign his tutorship. The Academy, under the control of the Coward Trustees, left Northampton in 1799 for Wymondley in Hertfordshire.

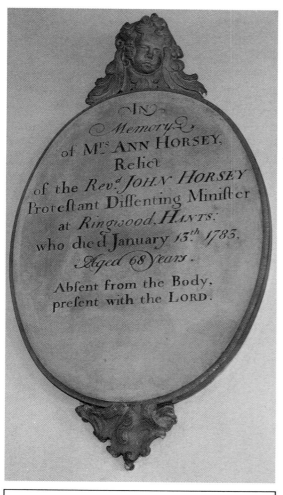

Ann Horsey's memorial at Castle Hill

It appears that Horsey's widowed mother, Ann, lived with them in Northampton and died on 13 January 1783. His late father, the Revd John Horsey, had been the Protestant Dissenting Minister at Ringwood, Hampshire. Horsey and his family occupied the 'Minister's House' at No 18 St Mary's Street which had been formerly two separate dwellings. As we have seen it was resolved to convert the property into a single dwelling and this seems to have been the object of major renovation work in 1799. Recently discovered tradesmen's bills give a fascinating insight into what was done. The whole property was extensively refurbished. Mr Mitchell's bill for retiling, replastering patches in the ceilings, staircase, kitchen and closets, limewashing the cellars and other redecorating cost £45. 10s. 2d. Mr Mason, the carpenter, charged £55. 13s. 11d. for taking down the old roof, making good the floors, fixing the brewhouse door, replacing cornices, putting in shelves and cupboards and fixing doors, fixing the 'dunghole and repairing the front door' and providing much Irish oak and ash and 'divers sorts of Nails & Spriggs, Iron rimmed hooks, spring catches & Thumb Catches and Turn buckles etc etc'. The mason's bill mentions his work from 1 April 1799 to 27th August of that year as he replaced stonework throughout the building, especially windows sills, and the erection of a new garden wall. One bill from a Mr Wilson amounted to £2. 17s. 6d. for providing forty-six gallons of ale for the workmen. Such lubrication seems to have the order of the days as most of the bills include a beer allowance for the men. The whole enterprise cost £186. 12s. 0d. Thus the church manse, redolent with a new slated roof instead of its old pantiles, having a stuccoed three storey front and gleaming with fresh paint faced the end of the year and the beginning of a new century. Horsey and his family continued to occupy 'the parsonage' until his death in 1827.

Doddridge had initiated a charity school for boys way back in 1738; this had had the backing of the Castle Hill Church and had probably survived until 1772. Doddridge's hopes of extending education to girls had not materialised. Yet a tradition had begun. By 1785 most children of the poor were employed for six days a week with only Sunday as a day off. Robert Raikes, the father of the great pioneer of the Sunday School Movement, had lived in Northampton and had been co-owner with William Dicey of the Northampton *Mercury*. From 1785 Sunday Schools were established across the land. Local churches began to co-operate in the provision of basic education; College Street Baptist Church and the Quaker Meeting in Kingswell Street co-operated with Castle Hill in a joint venture. Boys were educated in a cottage in Marefair; the tenant, a Mr Walker, managed proceedings and was compensated by two shillings a week for his time and trouble. Girls were not left out and a Mrs Coe conducted a school in Castle Street. Yet these ventures only succeeded in attracting less than two dozen children. But on 7 October 1810 the College Street Baptists began their own Sunday School, and at about the same time Castle Hill established its own Girls School under the leadership of Horsey's daughter together with Miss Taylor and Miss Haines. In 1810 some 220 children attended Sunday Schools in Northampton, 200 at All Saints and St Giles, and 20 at the Nonconformist Sunday schools. Within five years the numbers had risen to no less than 750 children of Northampton who were 'experiencing the transforming efficacy of moral and religious tuition'. In 1823 a Boys' School was founded by a Dr Clarke in a house occupied by a Mr Cornfield in St Mary's Street. Within two years the accommodation proved totally inadequate and the Castle Hill Church began to actively consider providing its own Sunday School premises. A School Building Committee was formed and met in the old vestry. The secretary was Thomas Grundy, an ironfounder, who provided drawings for a new building together with detailed estimates. It was specified that the building should be on two floors to accommodate girls upstairs and boys downstairs.

In January 1826 the church approached 'The Worshipful the Mayor and Corporation of the Town of Northampton' with the following appeal:

'The congregation of Protestant Dissenters assembled for Divine Worship at the Castle Hill Meeting House having formerly experienced the liberality of the Mayor and Corporation of Northampton in providing them with an additional piece of land for the purpose of enlarging the burial ground attached to the place, are again induced to trespass upon their kindness. For some years past they have supported a Sunday School for girls only, and lately a boys' school has been established which has increased beyond their most sanguine expectations, so that the room they have occupied has become too small to accommodate the additional members, it is therefore the intention of the congregation (should this request be complied with) to erect a new building two stories high of sufficient dimensions to receive the girls in the upper room, and the boys in the lower one. To enable them to accomplish this desirable object they beg leave therefore respectfully to solicit a further grant of land, adjoining the burying ground on the North side, which now forms the road, on which to erect a new school. Instead of the present roadway, they propose to remove part of the Castle Hill, to form a new one of the same width as the present road, to pass immediately in front of the proposed building...As the education of the children of the poor is the sole object the subscribers to this school have in view, they trust that no other statement is requisite to induce the Mayor and Corporation to grant this request, knowing that the establishment of Sunday Schools must be a principal means of preventing the increase of vice and immorality, and of promoting the interests of virtue and religion among the rapidly increasing population of this town'.

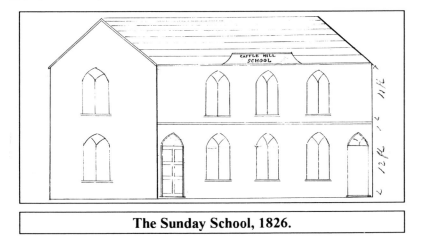

The Sunday School, 1826.

David Hewlet, the Mayor, and the Corporation gave the request sympathetic consideration and sold the church the necessary land. The new schools were built at a cost of £500, accommodated 300 children and were completed by March 1827. Sadly, the building of the schoolrooms was attended by a fatal accident; one of the workmen, a William Pettifer aged about 32, was killed when a great deal of rubble fell on him whilst removing part of the Castle Hill. It is interesting to note the social composition of those who became subscribers to the Sunday School: Thomas Clark (surgeon), Samuel Peach (woolstapler), Richard Hedge (leather seller), Edward Cotton (currier), George Russell (upholsterer), Samuel Walker (draper and tailor), William Causby (grocer), John Mawle (farmer), Thomas Grundy (ironfounder), William Wood (auctioneer), William Hemery Johnson (builder), Thomas Coles (corn factor), Joseph Cooper (tailor), James Harley (glazier), John Rudsdell (surgeon), Henry Dolby (stationer) and Miss Haynes.

On 8 May 1825 Horsey's wife Hannah died aged 72 years. This, undoubtedly, had a profound effect upon him as he, too, was ailing in health. The following May was the fiftieth anniversary of his ordination to the Castle Hill pastorate; we do not know how this unique period of service was celebrated. By September 1826 Horsey was manifestly very ill and the pulpit had to be supplied by others. He half-heartedly tried to resign his charge. `To the Gentlemen composing the Committee for obtaining supplies for the Castle Hill Society' he wrote: `...the bodily indisposition with which providence has afflicted me seems to yield nothing to medical treatment, nor, perhaps, can we reasonably hope for more than a restoration to occasional service. The uncertainty of which requires something decisive to be done'. He wondered whether to resign or not but left `the matter to your superior judgement'. Their reply was to agree that `Mr Horsey should be continued in the pastorate, and receive his usual salary till after Christmas, when probably some alteration might be found necessary'.

Minutes regarding the Sunday school, 1826.

With their pastor out of action it was resolved to ensure that church life kept going. On New Year's Day 1827 it was agreed that `the Sunday School children should attend the public services in the Meeting House alternately, the boys on one part of the day, and the girls on the other. Mr Walker was requested to inform the Superintendent of the Girls' School of the wishes of the committee in this respect, leaving the choice of attending with the girls either in the morning or the afternoon'.

A letter was sent to Mr Morell, principal of the Wymondley Academy for suitable students to fill the vacant pulpit. Three names were suggested and young Charles Hyatt, ` a youth of great excellence, eminent piety, and one who, if spared, will prove a valuable pastor and useful minister' came to preach for the four Sundays from 28 January 1827. It was clear by the end of January that Horsey could not continue so on the 29th a letter was written to him by John Wood and Richard Hedge, deacons, expressing the heartfelt concern of the church:

`...after the most mature deliberation the church and committee of subscribers think that the present welfare and future prosperity of the interest at Castle Hill, as well as your own comfort and peace of mind, will be best promoted by your adopting the last of those plans which you proposed for the consideration of the committee, namely, resigning entirely that charge which you have so honourably filled, the rewards of which we trust you will receive at the hands of Him to whom all must give account of their stewardship...'.

Memorial to Revd John Horsey & Mrs Hannah Horsey at Castle Hill.

The church resolved to pay Horsey £50 per annum for life and to let him reside in the manse as long as necessary. The letter was not given to him until 17 March as his caring deacons did not want to give him further anxiety. After a brief rally of his health he relapsed and died on 12 May 1827 just one day short of fifty-one years as pastor of the church. His funeral was conducted by the Revd L. B. Edwards at the Castle Hill Church where he is buried with his wife. Horsey was not given to literary output although he published several sermons, and a volume of *Lectures to Young Persons* appeared a year after his death.

Revd Charles Hyatt 1827 - 1833

Revd Charles Hyatt

Charles Hyatt proved to be an acceptable preacher at Castle Hill. His initial four weeks pulpit supply was extended by four more, and then for a further four months as a candidate for the co-pastorship. By that time Horsey was dead and the serious consideration of fulfilling the vacancy was occupying the church's mind. Hyatt's father, also Charles Hyatt, started his working life as a shoemaker but had become the minister of the Ebenezer Chapel in Shadwell, London. Hyatt was ordained to the pastoral office at Castle Hill on Wednesday 26 September 1827. He recorded his thoughts of the occasion as the Northamptonshire Dissenting Ministers, in the town ready for their half-yearly gathering the following day, attended the service. The Revd William Gray of College Street took part in the ordination.` It was a most delightful and interesting service', Hyatt wrote, `nearly fifty ministers were present and the impressions then made will, it is hoped, never wear away'.

Although he was only twenty-two years of age and fresh from his six years at Wymondley the younger Hyatt's six years and three months' ministry were to serve the church well in cleaning out a persistent problem which had remained in the church since the time of Hextal. Although

Hyatt was of a tender and amiable disposition he knew where he stood on theological matters. Under his predecessor's mild unchallenging preaching the heresy of Arianism and its close cousin Unitarianism had existed within the congregation. It had been cross-fertilised by student preaching from the Academy, whether in Northampton, Daventry or Wymondley, as even the tutors were at variance over theological doctrines. Joseph Priestley, the famed natural philosopher and scientist was himself a product of the Daventry Academy and attested to the divergence of views. It was thus into difficulties that Charles Hyatt walked when on Friday 2 November 1827 he faced his first church meeting. A letter was read out as follows:

'To the Church of Christ Assembling under the pastoral Care of the Rev. C. Hyatt. We, the undersigned Members of the Church of Christ, assembling in Castle Hill Meeting, having, in obedience to the dictates of our consciences, united in the formation of a society of Christians, whose worship is directed solely to the one God, the Father, agreeably to the express injunctions of our Saviour, deem it proper to withdraw; and hereby beg leave to announce our withdrawment from the worship and communion of the Church to which we have hitherto belonged, on account of the discordance existing between the mode of worship as there practised, and that which we believe to have been enjoined and observed by Christ and his apostles'.

Nine people signed the letter: Sarah Haynes, Margaret Cotton, Ann Horsey (John Horsey's daughter), Ann Wish, Thomas Jones, William Causby, E.Causby, Thomas Lawrence and Henry A. Dalby. They promptly seceded from the church. The *Church Book* notes: 'The individuals whose withdrawment is here announced have in connection with some of the Subscribers formed themselves into a Society professing Unitarian principles'. With money given them from a wealthy sympathiser and support from the Unitarian Association they refurbished the old Wesleyan Chapel in King Street where they met for worship. 'They had left the meadow for the common'(AC180). It was, however, an essential blood-letting that cleared out the proverbial stables and made way for a sounder church fellowship. 'There [were] no signs of noisy enthusiasm, no wrought up revival; the ministry [of Hyatt] was calm, thoughtful, deliberate, and the church had the grace of spiritual rest, the rest of well ordered movement' (AC182).

In spite of the membership having declined to some fifty people, its lowest ebb, there was still sufficient spirituality in the church under firm leadership for a revival to take place. On 14 January 1829 the church meeting reasserted the principles of its foundation:

'The church anxious for the maintenance of their discipline and for the promotion of its spiritual prosperity unanimously adopted the following resolution.
I That we solemnly renew the covenant into which this Church entered in the year 1694 upon the settlement of the Rev Mr Shepherd amongst them.
II That as a congregational Church we have the right to make such laws as we deem best for the discipline and management of the body so far as they do not directly or indirectly violate any of the laws of Christ.
III That as a distinct and separate body we claim to ourselves the power of determining upon every thing that involves the interests of the Society, and we do resolve according to the principles of the New Testament the general order of Congregational Churches & the practice of our own Church in former times to maintain our right to the management & direction of all affairs temporal as well as spiritual to the rejection of all foreign interference from any individual or body of individuals whatever.
IV That recognising the authority of Pastor & Deacons as those offices are exercised among Congregational Dissenters the one relating to spiritual the other to temporal affairs we willingly engage to obey them that rule over us in the Lord & submit to their authority so far as it is exercised according to the laws of Christ the Great Head of the Church.
V That acknowledging the truth of the Psalmist's words: "Behold how good & how pleasant it is for brethren to dwell together in unity", we take the new commandment of Christ that we love one another even as he hath loved us as the rule of our conduct to each other & promise to endeavour to live in peace with all men especially with those who are of the household of faith.
VI That perceiving the impossibility of recording all the cases in which discipline is to be exercised & considering that the New Testament is sufficiently explicit upon the subject we leave the determination of it

to the occurrence of circumstances resolving to be governed in our decisions by the former practices of our Church & the laws of Jesus Christ.

VII   That no Church Meeting can be summoned without the previous knowledge of the Pastor & Deacons.
VIII   That the vote of the majority is the voice of the Church'.

The statement carries the signatures of Hyatt, his two deacons (John Wood and Richard Hedge) and the signatures or marks of forty-six members, virtually the entire membership of the church. An addendum notes that even members who were not able to be present at the meeting had heartedly agreed with the resolutions. Hyatt, young as he was, had united the church around him and had given the death blow to the trouble that had embroiled Hextal and had been too incipient for the easy-going Horsey to tackle, namely the problem of others who had wealth, influence and loud voices who sought to overrule the Christ-centred focus of the church meeting. Before the close of that church meeting another resolution found unanimous support:

'That the appointment of a Committee during the illness of the late pastor to engage supplies and manage the affairs of the Society be not considered as any precedent for future times and that we consider that the only ground on which such an appointment can be justified was the peculiar nature of the circumstances in which the Church was then placed'.

It was clear that no longer would the tail wag the dog. A new spirit was let loose in the church and from that time membership steadily rose, some hundred members being added to the church in Hyatt's relatively brief ministry of six years and three months. One new member of the church, a Miss Russell is mentioned; beside her name the pastor has added proudly `now Mrs Hyatt'. As part of the general growth of the church it was necessary to increase the diaconate; in July 1831 upon John Wood's retirement because of infirmity the church unanimously elected Mr Mason, Mr Coles, Mr Hagger and Mr Putley to fill the office as deacons.

A significant indication of the church's renewed sense of well-being came in 1830 when a branch Sunday School was formed in a cottage in St James' End. Separated from the town by a moor, in winter by floods, wild and neglected, St James' End was shunned as a disreputable and even a dangerous place. It had no religious service of any sort. Only two houses existed beyond the *Green Man* public house, where tolls were collected on goods coming into the town. No lamps existed beyond Black Lion Hill and women would wait at the town end of the narrow West Bridge for company before venturing across. Fear of robbery was constant. J. J. Cooper noted that `the bulls of St James' End often roared, and to open a Sunday School there was a

daring deed, but it asserted its right and justified its claim'(AC183). The cottage belonged to Mr Watts, a member at Castle Hill, and this early attempt to bring Christian teaching to St James met with considerable local success. However, after three years the venture was to be discontinued with Watts being paid half a year's rent for his cottage on 24 June 1833. Seventeen years later the project was revived with considerable results.

Another mark of the church's outgoing nature at this time is seen in the willing `dismission' of Mrs Abel, from the church to become one of the foundation members of a new church being erected in Commercial Street. Mrs Abel joined seven others from King Street in the joint venture of beginning a new outreach.

Commercial Street Congregational Church, erected 1828, closed 1959.

Under the leadership of the Revd Edmund Prust who was ordained to his charge on 21 April 1830 the new church began. Prust was to give to Northampton a ministry of fifty years and rich in blessings.

On 31 March 1833 Hyatt preached for the last time at Castle Hill. He had received a unanimous invitation from his father's church at Shadwell in London. His father had laboured there for twenty-nine years and needed an able assistant with the work of ministering to seamen. The younger Hyatt commenced work there with enthusiasm becoming superintendent of the Seamen's Mission. In 1844 he was appointed secretary to the *British and Foreign Sailors' Society*. Never possessed of a robust constitution Hyatt felt the strain of taking over his ailing father's work. In June 1846 his father died followed by his son only nine months later. Yet Hyatt had built faithfully and well and in Northampton he had laid foundations which were to provide the essential supports for considerable expansion as the nineteenth century unfolded.

Revd John Bennett 1833 - 1859

Revd John Bennett

Soon after Charles Hyatt's resignation the Revd John Bennett from Braunton in Devonshire visited the church to preach. His services met with general approval and he was duly called to the pastorate. Aged thirty Bennett came with some trepidation to the Castle Hill pulpit. The son of a soldier and born in Wellington, Somersetshire, he had been educated in barrack schools and was self-conscious at his less polished educational attainments than his predecessor. Nevertheless, he had other qualities of experience and devotion to Christian evangelism. As an agent for the Home Missionary Society he had accepted the responsibility of seven villages and three Sunday schools in the Braunton area, walking his thirty-mile rounds and ministering to the rural community. Under Hyatt's influence Castle Hill Church was a strong supporter of the Home Missionary Society, subscribing between £30 and £40 per annum in its support. Hyatt had visited the Society's West Country venture some five years earlier, undoubtedly making the acquaintance of Bennett. Thus Castle Hill and its next minister had been introduced.

On 11 July 1833 John Bennett signified his acceptance of the Call to Castle Hill. He was glad that out of a membership of 106 nearly ninety had signed the letter of invitation and others not present had also signified their agreement. He saw in the situation, which was *'not in any degree of my seeking ...the finger of God. From Him I have humbly and earnestly entreated counsel and direction, and I feel firmly persuaded that in the step I am about to take I am but going where the Lord has called me'*. Bennett set about his ministry with energy and quickly gained the respect and affection of young and old. Within the first year of his ministry his heart was gladdened to see Thomas Lord of the Castle Hill congregation entering the Christian ministry at Wollaston and later Brigstock. Lord was the first of four young men whom Bennett encouraged and trained to be ministers of the Gospel. He likewise encouraged three of his members to be engaged in village preaching. His experience of rural poverty in Somersetshire made Bennett a fierce advocate for social justice. *'With a fluent tongue, a powerful voice, a popular address, he was one of the forces of the town and had to be reckoned with on public questions, for he inspired enthusiasm in the cause he advocated. To those who did not know him he seemed fiery and even fierce, but there was neither wrath nor venom in his nature, he was one of the most humble-minded men that ever lived'* (AC188).

Bennett was married in Castle Hill Church on 26 September 1837 to a Miss Taylor, a maiden lady who carried on a business in the town. This was a significant occasion as it marked the very first legal marriage ceremony to be authorised in any Nonconformist place of worship in the town. The registration certificate, signed by William Tomalin, superintendent registrar, declares: 'the Building named Castle Hill Chapel situated at Castle Hills in the Parish of Saint Peter having been duly certified as a place of Public religious worship, was registered for the Solemnisation of Marriage therein, on the eighteenth day of August in the Year of our Lord one thousand eight hundred and thirty-seven'.

The Castle Hill Sunday School took part in the local celebrations of the coronation of Queen Victoria in June 1838. The *Mercury* reported:

'Perhaps the most interesting spectacle was that of the Sunday School Children. About 1500 belonging to the Church were assembled in the barrack yard and liberally regaled with plum cake and tea; and an equal or rather greater number of children, trained by the Dissenters, formed in the Market Square and proceeding to Mr Hagger's brewery were entertained in a similar manner. Each division carried banners suitably inscribed, and before parting sang the National Anthem and two or three other pieces'.

1851 saw the centenary of the death of Philip Doddridge. It was decided to hold the Autumnal Meetings of the Congregational Union in Northampton in order to gain inspiration from such an occasion. The organisers' hopes were profoundly realised; the Revd. Dr. John Stoughton 'spoke with such fervid eloquence that the whole assembly was strangely impressed, and many strong men were melted to tears'. Together with the other two Congregational ministers in the town, the Revd E.T. Prust of Commercial Street and the Rev G. Nicholson of King Street, Bennett was warmly thanked for his part in the proceedings of the assembly. It was a time of upward movement of the spirit. Together with stalwart members of the congregation like Jonathan Robinson and Pickering Phipps Perry, two indefatigable deacons, Bennett presided over a church that grew in numerical strength to 160 with a still larger number of young people.

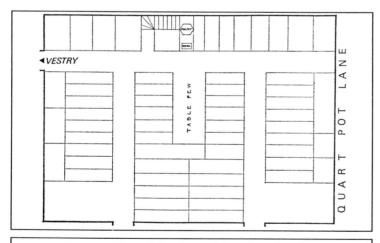

Thomas Grundy's plan of the church, 1826.

During these years the first major alterations to the old Meeting House were made. In 1839 extensive repairs were carried out on the lower portions of the building. Lobbies were constructed for the gallery stairs so that stone replaced the open wooden treads that ascended 'in the sight of all Israel'. New aisles were added. By 1852 new galleries were constructed, and the two ancient pillars, 'Jachin and Boaz'(one of them described as 'a little bandy') were taken out as the entire roof was replaced. Only the walls and the vestry of the original Meeting House were left. A plan drawn by Thomas Grundy in 1826 gives detail of the interior of the church clearly showing the box pew around which the Academy students sat to make their notes on the sermons and the conduct of services. Although the pulpit and pewing of the galleries were still untouched from Doddridge's time in 1851 it is most likely that the box pew survived until the 1862 alterations.

It was during this time that the evangelical fervour of the church began to find expression in outreach in St James' End. A deserted blacksmith's shop standing at the corner of Mill Road became the premises of a Sunday School in 1850. For some thirteen years a small band of teachers managed to maintain regular instruction for upward of seventy boys and girls (the two sexes being separated in the room by a single

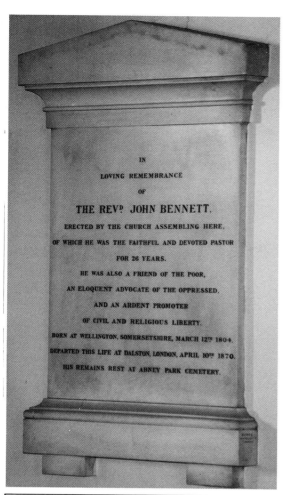

IN

LOVING REMEMBRANCE

OF

THE REV^D JOHN BENNETT.

ERECTED BY THE CHURCH ASSEMBLING HERE,

OF WHICH HE WAS THE FAITHFUL AND DEVOTED PASTOR

FOR 26 YEARS.

HE WAS ALSO A FRIEND OF THE POOR,

AN ELOQUENT ADVOCATE OF THE OPPRESSED,

AND AN ARDENT PROMOTER

OF CIVIL AND RELIGIOUS LIBERTY.

BORN AT WELLINGTON, SOMERSETSHIRE, MARCH 12TH 1804.

DEPARTED THIS LIFE AT DALSTON, LONDON, APRIL 10TH 1870.

HIS REMAINS REST AT ABNEY PARK CEMETERY.

Memorial to Revd John Bennett at Castle Hill

curtain) until more adequate premises were provided. It was the forerunner of massive expansion as the century drew to its close.

Bennett's health began to suffer and he became subject to severe nervous depression. During 1858 the Revd Charles Horne, father of the Revd Silvester Horne, was called to be assistant pastor; he fulfilled his duties until the end of the year. Realising that he could not continue Bennett resigned his charge with great sorrow of heart. The church members presented him with a retirement gift of £500. He left Northampton for Slough, later removing to Dalston where he died after a long and painful illness on 10 April 1870 at the age of sixty-six. He had faithfully built for a quarter of a century upon the work of Hyatt; Castle Hill Church was poised to reap the harvest of the expansion of Nonconformity in the latter part of the nineteenth century.

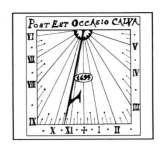

Part 5
1860 - 1904
The ministries of Arnold, Oates, Cooper and Davie

Revd Thomas Arnold: 1860 - 1882

Revd Thomas Arnold

The search for a suitable successor to John Bennett created something of a crisis for the church in the eighteen months between January 1859 and June 1860. Several possible ministers were invited to preach but for a variety of reasons the pastoral vacancy remained. The church was on the point of inviting the Revd Benjamin Beddow of Barnsley to be the next minister when unexpected news was received that the Revd Thomas Arnold had arrived in England, having travelled from Australia via the Holy Land. Arnold had already excited intense interest and `the strong desire formerly expressed to hear him was renewed & the Committee...requested to hear him preach at the earliest opportunity'(BG56).

Thomas Arnold's family traced itself back to a Puritan settler who was one of three brothers serving in the army of William III in Ireland. Arnold's parents were Moravians and lived in the settlement at Gracehill, County Antrim. In his youth he had taught in the Gracehill school before moving to Manchester as a town missionary. Later he moved to Doncaster where he taught at the Yorkshire Deaf-Mute Institute. After joining the Congregational Church he became a student at Rotherham College during which time he took on a student-pastorate at the English Church in Hamburg. After college he held pastorates at Burton-on-Trent and Smethwick before accepting a call to the church at Balmain, Sydney, New South Wales. In Australia he developed his interest in the teaching of deaf mutes. However, serious illness caused his doctor to advise his return to England, which he did; his arrival during the summer of 1860 caused much excitement at Northampton. On 20 June the church sent a letter to him at Newcastle-upon-Tyne signed by 136 members: `[we] most earnestly and cordially invite you to take the spiritual oversight of our church and congregation'. He replied on the 30th that he had `great defects and great unworthiness, but if we are sincere and determined to be governed solely by the gracious spirit of our religion, all these will speedily be overlooked, and God will magnify Himself among us by the conversion of many, and the growth of all in goodness and holiness'. He hoped that `we might journey together towards heaven, and persuade many to go with us'. His ministry began on 19 August 1860 and was soon followed by signs of spiritual awakening.

In his first sermon preached on behalf of the Sunday Schools on 30 September 1860 Arnold encouraged action in recruiting more children. On 2 October, upon his initiative, the teachers began a systematic visitation of the area with the view of increasing the number of pupils. In 1861 Miss Martha Burton was engaged as a Bible woman, or Scripture reader, and a committee of ladies was formed to superintend her work. Four years later another Bible woman, a Mrs Jones from Desborough, was appointed to work in the St James' area where the Sunday School, recommenced in 1850 in the old smithy, had been transferred in 1862 to a new building purposely erected as a school-chapel. When this opened on 1 January 1863 the number of children attending immediately doubled. Encouraged by this it was resolved to 'carry on an evening service at St James' New School by the aid of the members of [Doddridge] Church'. Within a few years the entire cost of the St James Bible woman's work was taken on by P.P.Perry and his wife on behalf of the Castle Hill Church. By 1871 this branch of the church had become so successful that £236 was spent on the purchase of a plot of land adjoining the school-chapel. It was on this ground that the Doddridge Memorial Church was to be built.

The work in St James was paralleled by similar efforts in the expanding area of Kingsthorpe Hollow on the north side of the town. The work began with an outreach as a Sunday School. Conducted by a Miss J. Morton, who lodged with the minister's family at that time, the school soon attracted numerous children. Arnold had taken on the work on his own initiative hiring a couple of rooms in a cottage in July 1865 and single-handedly continuing the work until it became officially adopted as a branch school of Castle Hill Chapel. Mrs Arnold had commenced a mothers' meeting. In October the teachers resolved:

That this meeting being of opinion that the Sunday School instituted by the Rev. T. Arnold and carried on in a cottage near Primrose Hill during the last three months, and already containing forty children, should be adopted as one of Doddridge Chapel branch schools, strongly recommends that its recognition be urged upon the Church at their next meeting'.

By the following March a Mr Curtis was elected as superintendent 'with liberty to expend 10 shillings for the purchase of school requisites'. Fifty-six scholars were by then attending of whom eight could read the scriptures and a similar number attended day school. Within six months the flourishing new branch school had difficulties in finding enough accommodation. Enquiries were being made for 'a whole cottage to be appropriated for the purpose of the school', but it proved too costly. Curtis was succeeded by James Robertson. Accommodation was provided by renting rooms in various cottages in the neighbourhood until in 1870 Mr Henry Dingle's house at 17 Arthur Street was acquired and used both as a preaching station and school. This was to result in the formation of the Primrose Hill Congregational Church in 1903.

With developments proceeding apace at St James' End and Primrose Hill the centre of operations at Castle Hill was itself in dire need of expansion. Congregations had grown and the old chapel desperately needed enlarging. Some considered pulling it down and rebuilding or even erecting a new chapel on a new site, but Arnold wisely realised the church's historic heritage and pressed for sympathetic development. Thus in 1862 the chapel was enlarged, the north wall being demolished and the eastern and western walls extended across the open space used for burials between it and the Sunday School building. Some three hundred additional places were provided within the chapel thus raising its seating capacity to some nine hundred and fifty. By 1878 the Sunday School buildings had been enlarged, increasing the capacity to over a thousand places. The times called for new initiatives; a rapidly expanding population and religious revival called for new expressions of devotion and faith. It was at this moment that the name of the church was changed from Castle Hill to what was considered the 'more definite and more appropriate name of *Doddridge* Chapel'. Quart Pot Lane was also being renamed Doddridge Street, considered more fitting than the name of a local public house. All the church's building developments, costing £3018, were paid from subscriptions and of the surplus it was willingly agreed to give the minister £73. 10s for his exertions and £21 to John Bennett 'who had recently suffered the bereavement of his youngest daughter and for this and other causes had been brought very low'.

The Sunday School at *Doddridge* continued to grow; with growth came the problems of recruiting sufficient teachers. On 19 November 1883 one hundred and forty parents and friends sat down to tea in the upper schoolroom presided over by the minister. He commented that the work of the Sunday School teacher was one of 'the grandest works upon which anyone could be engaged'. During the meeting Mr Abel commented favourably on the proposal of closing public houses on Sundays; it would, he remarked, help the unpunctuality problem amongst the scholars due to fathers coming home late from the public houses for Sunday dinner and the children having to wait for theirs.

Arnold was a minister with clear ideas as to the direction of his ministry. The church agreed to pay him a minimum of £200 per annum rising in proportion as the congregation grew. He and his wife were to live at *Fair View*, Cliftonville and so the church manse could be rented out in order to offset his stipend. He was to have five weeks 'vacation' a year with 'the church to bear the expense of supplying the pulpit in my absence'. The church 'cheerfully and unanimously' agreed to 'the intended mode of his ministry'. The church meeting of 31 October 1860 soon saw its direction with changes to the days of church meetings, the moving of the Lord's Supper to after the morning service rather than the afternoon, the readmission of lapsed members into the church and the stipulation that those who absent themselves 'from the Lord's Table for four consecutive months, without furnishing satisfactory reason, shall be considered as self-excluded'. Visitation of absent members was stepped up and visitors appointed to interview enquirers for membership. Month by month the *Church Book* records the steady build up of new members, many newcomers to the town. Overall membership rose during Arnold's ministry from 136 to 293, the most significant growth in over a century.

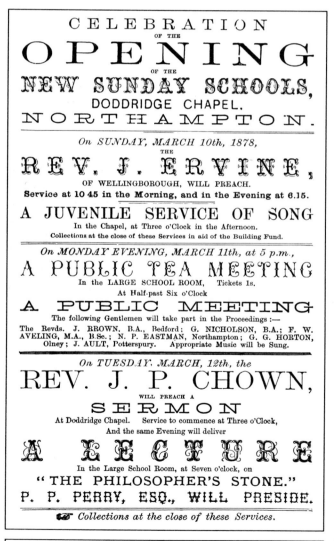

Notice for the opening of the new Sunday School 1878

During Arnold's ministry it became customary to have an annual *Financial Statement* for the preceding year published in which articles on church history and life were featured. The statement for 1882, the year of his retirement, shows the vigorous and varied life of the church. Preaching was organised not only at Doddridge but at St James End and Kingsthorpe Road, ten and six preachers respectively in each of the last two places. Sunday Schools operated at all three places totalling 87 teachers and 1098 scholars. At Doddridge there was a Bible Class, a Young Men's Literary Society, a Band of Hope (also at St James' End and Kingsthorpe Road), a Female Bible Mission at both Doddridge and St James' End, a Mothers' Meeting at Kingsthorpe Road, a Doddridge Chapel Clothing Society, a Doddridge Chapel Maternal Meeting, a Doddridge Chapel Ladies Dorcas Society, a Sea Side fund at Doddridge, Clothing Clubs at all three places plus other numerous organisations supporting such ventures as the London Missionary Society, the County Infirmary, the Village Preachers' Association, the English Congregational Church Building Society and the Town Mission. Apart from January and June special monthly collections were made for these good causes in turn. The minister was backed up by eight deacons, a church secretary and a Chapel Committee of eighteen. Services were held on Sundays at 11am and 6.30pm. Sunday School at 9.30am and 2.30pm.and a Sunday Prayer Meeting at 7.45pm. On Mondays there were the Mothers' Meeting, the Clothing Club, Prayer Meeting and Bible Class. Tuesdays saw the Literary Society Meeting, Wednesdays a Prayer Meeting and Lecture, alternate Thursdays the Band of Hope, and Saturdays a Prayer Meeting for the Young. In addition to these activities every month saw a Church Meeting, a Sunday School Prayer Meeting, a Sacramental Service, a Missionary Prayer Meeting, a Ladies' Working Meeting and a Maternal Meeting. At quarterly intervals a Baptismal Service for children was held on the second Sunday immediately after the morning service. A special quarterly Afternoon Service for the Young was also held and also Special Week-Day Services for the Young on the third Wednesday. Every six months the church gathered for a Tea Meeting as did the Teachers.

There is no doubt that Nonconformity was lubricated by 'chapel tea' and the Doddridge Chapel was no exception. A feature of its life was the tea meeting which frequently started at 6pm and was then followed by the church meeting. One such significant meeting was held on 6 October 1862:

'On Monday evening October 6th 1862 a Public Tea Meeting was held at the New School Rooms, Castle Hill or Doddridge Chapel, the name by which it will henceforth be also known. Between Four and Five Hundred persons were present. About half past six an adjournment took place to the Chapel which presently became quite full. Mr P.P.Perry took the Chair. The meeting was addressed by Rev Williams (Baptist Minister of Hackleton), Jas. Brown (Cemetery), Smith (Harpole) Geo. Nicholson (minister of King St.) and Rev T. Arnold...the trays being gratuitously provided by the ladies...net result £72.11s.6d'.

Arnold involved himself in the pastoral problems of his growing congregation and the *Church Book* records instances when he needed tact and discretion in handling difficult situations. One such was the case of a certain couple within the church who had been engaged to be married, and the wedding day fixed. *'On the day previous [to the wedding] he [the husband-to-be] left a note intimating an alteration of mind. This [is] stated to be the fourth time he has practised a similar deception on one member or another of the fair sex'.* The man in question was suspended from church membership for three months and *'further enquiries [were] made'.*

Ever since his days in Doncaster Thomas Arnold kept alive his deep interest in the plight of deaf-mutes. Whilst in Australia he resumed his work in this field returning to England with a pupil whom he virtually adopted as a son. Others were to join the Arnold household under the motherly care of Mrs Arnold and the wise tutorship of her husband. For fifteen years until his retirement from the Castle Hill pastorate on 1 July 1882 Arnold ceaselessly evinced his practical interest in the education of deaf mutes. His retirement from the pastorate gave him more time to devote to his school. This was taken over subsequently by Hugh Neville Dixon who assisted him both in the church and the school. Arnold was the first in England to apply the pure oral system of educating deaf mutes. The London College of Deaf Mute Teachers honoured him with a diploma and encouraged him to write a teaching manual which became a standard textbook on the subject. He also published a history of the teaching of deaf mutes in various parts of the world. As part of his researches he taught himself French, German, Italian and Spanish, the last being learned after he was 70 years of age.

Arnold's political interests were decidedly Liberal, as were most Nonconformists, and he fought the atheist member of parliament Charles Bradlaugh with unflinching determination. Arnold was of 'striking intellectual appearance', notes the *Chronicle* obituary on 21 January 1897:

'He was one of the most eloquent preachers and platform orators Northampton ever possessed, his language being as lucid as it was ornate, whilst his elocutionary powers were exceptionally fine. Of kindly disposition and sunny characteristics, he gladdened and brightened every circle in which he moved: and the child and the veteran were alike happy to see and hear him'.

Such affection was evident in the final presentation to Mr & Mrs Arnold upon his retirement on 15 June 1882:

'After a Public tea, at which 400 attended, the Public Meeting was held in the Chapel, at half-past Six o'Clock. The platform was crowded by Ministers from the town and county, and the Chapel well filled with the Members of the Congregation and other friends of all denominations who wished to do honour to the retiring Pastor'.

Revd John Oates

Gifts presented to them on behalf of the church by Jonathan Robinson included a purse of £450 'as an expression of their gratitude for, and admiration of, his unwearied ministrations, loving service, and consistent life' over some twenty-two years as pastor. A magnificent timepiece and an illuminated address from the deacons, a handsome Davenport and easy chair for Mrs Arnold plus other gifts were overwhelming manifestations of the warmth of the people for their pastor and his wife.

Feeling that the burdens of the pastorate were becoming too much for Arnold the church appointed **the Revd John Oates as co-pastor in 1878.** Born in South Africa of English Methodist parents John Oates took an early delight in helping teach in the Mission Sunday School. He became a well-respected preacher in the diamond fields before being accepted as a student for the ministry by the Congregational Union of South Africa. He was sent to New College, London for his training. He pursued a brilliant academic course being Wardlaw Exhibitioner and Kendal-Binney Prizeman. He was on the point of returning to South Africa when the Call to the co-pastorate at Castle Hill was sent to him. Like Thomas Arnold, Oates was beloved of his people, and both men worked in harmony for almost four years until the former's retirement. There was no hesitation in the church calling Oates to the sole-pastorship after Arnold's departure. He was ordained to his charge on 2 March 1882. It was a great disappointment to the church that after a year he resigned the pastorate. He accepted the charge of a church in Reading (which he considerably enlarged) and in 1889 moved on to Christ Church (Congregational) Reading. Of his sermons preached and published an outstanding example is one delivered at the Town Hall on behalf of the Y.M.C.A. in January 1880 on the Pilgrim Fathers.

After his retirement from Castle Hill Thomas Arnold continued in the town with his work with the deaf and dumb and as an elder statesman within Nonconformity. It was from his house, 27 St Paul's Road, that his funeral cortege left for the funeral at Castle Hill on Monday 25th January 1897. He was eighty years old. The chapel was crowded and the white and gold pulpit was heavily draped in black. The impressive service was commenced with a reading by the Rev Thomas Gasquoine followed by an address by Arnold's successor, the Rev J. J. Cooper. Other ministers took part. The cortege of nineteen horse-drawn coaches including relatives, officers of the church, the Mayor and others proceeded along Doddridge Street, Marefair and Gold Street to the Billing Road Cemetery. Many were unable to be present due to the bitter cold weather, snow storms and the slushy streets. *The Daily Reporter* for 25 January 1897 commented:

Memorial to Revd Thomas Arnold and Sarah Arnold at Castle Hill.

`...when the life of Mr Arnold comes to be written, and his work appreciated, it will be seen that he holds one of the foremost places in Northampton's history. Mr Arnold is one of the few men whose influence will be felt in succeeding generations. In his own special line, the education of deaf mutes, he had no peer. As a minister and as a man he is already appreciated, and so there crowded into Doddridge Chapel yesterday afternoon old members of his church during his ministry, younger members who delighted to hear him when he occasionally occupied the pulpit, personal friends, fellow ministers, former pupils, teachers of the deaf and dumb - all came in sorrow round his bier. All felt that a great man had gone to his reward'.

The Times noted: `Possessed of very considerable intellectual activity and rare culture, a born thinker, philosopher, and teacher, he was a man of ideas and ideals'.

Revd Joseph J. Cooper: 1884 - 1904

Revd Joseph J. Cooper

The year 1884 began with no clear prospect of an early settlement of a pastor. A Call was issued to the Revd Hope Davison of London who had preached at Castle Hill during February and March. The death of his wife after a short illness forced him to decline the offer; the church meeting of 31 March sent its condolences intimating its willingness to wait for Mr Davison but on 24 April the deacons received his profound regret at being unable to come to Northampton.

It was not until the Chapel Anniversary on 28 September that the Revd Joseph J. Cooper of Corwen occupied the pulpit. Whilst holidaying at Penmaenmawr in July the Revd Thomas Arnold had heard him preach and saw in him a worthy successor. The church members found him `eminently qualified permanently to occupy the pulpit, and minister within the venerable walls where the sainted Doddridge so faithfully and successfully laboured'. A special church meeting on 22 October followed by meetings on the 29th and after the evening service on 5 November sent a unanimous call hoping that they would have `the unspeakable pleasure of welcoming you as our pastor and friend'. Cooper replied on 10 November confirming his acceptance. `I steadfastly believe', he wrote, `when God calls a servant to work that he either finds or gives the needed power. I shall bring you a whole heart, and as God shall help me, a devoted spirit'. On 11 December the Revd J. J. Cooper was publicly recognised as the pastor of the church. Some 500 people welcomed him at a public tea in the large schoolroom. His ministry began on the first Sunday of the New Year, 1885.

Cooper had been born at King's Lynn in Norfolk in 1837. His father was a Primitive Methodist minister. Cooper was early apprenticed to a carpenter and spent his youthful days in Sunday School teaching and as an `exhorter' on the Primitive Methodist Society's preaching `plan'. He moved to London to follow his trade and became an assistant to ministers who had been forced to rest from their work due to illness; he workd in Eynesbury (Huntingdonshire), Maidstone and Chelmsford. He eventually transferred his allegiance to the Congregational Church and went to Weston-super-Mare under the auspices of the London Missionary Society to study under the Revd C. Pritchett. Being ordained at Chelmsford in 1865 he was sent to British Guiana.

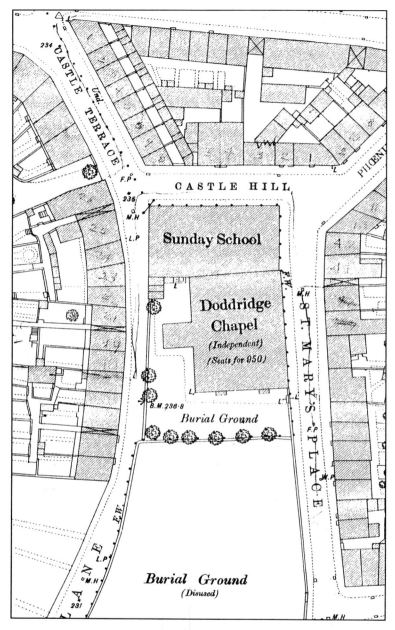

The breakdown of his wife's health and his own made them return to Britain. A period of lecturing, travelling and preaching followed until he settled at Corwen where he ministered to a small and appreciative congregation. Arnold's chance meeting in July 1884 changed the course of his life and added another significant chapter to the story of Castle Hill.

The immediate area around the church comprised houses built before 1846. The development of industry in Northampton, particularly the boot and shoe trade, resulted in the building of numerous terraced houses in order to accommodate the burgeoning population. Consequently there was a shift away from the town centre to the developing suburbs of the wealthier, church-going families. The immediate area around the church housed a section of society which knew poverty, the pawnshop and the public house. It was to this altered scene that the church needed to address its mission. In J. J. Cooper they had a minister well able to lead into new ventures. By October 1885 handbills were being circulated around the area encouraging attendance at `a special service for Working Men and Women'. In the autumn of 1888 the Doddridge and King Street chapels, together with other Free Churches, united in an evangelical mission which involved neighbourhood visiting and open-air services. It had a remarkable effect on the area and many young people `expressed their desire to consecrate themselves to the service of Christ'.

The locality of the church in 1885, surrounded by houses and adjacent to the old St Mary's burial ground.

Cooper's ministry centred itself on evangelical principles. In January 1889 he stressed the importance of another mission that would `be more likely to reach the masses who are not in the habit of attending any place of worship'. He was keen to encourage `cottage missions' where people used their homes as vehicles of outreach, and open air meetings. In 1901, after a massive mission involving all the Free Churches of the town Cooper addressed the large gathering at College Street Baptist Church upon its conclusion; such a mission was a new method for a new century, he urged, and hoped that the weaknesses of the churches in not visiting their neighbourhoods, now that agreement had been made to dividing the town into districts, would be remedied.

Cooper upbraided his church of some 350 members for the poor attendance at the frequent prayer meetings held at the church and constantly challenged his congregation to build up their own spiritual life. Annually the *Practical Precepts* of the church were published and Cooper unremittingly remindered his people of their importance:

1. Remember that you do not come to the sanctuary as hearers much less as spectators, but as worshippers. There is danger in these days of subordinating every part of public worship to the sermon. Come, not only hungering for the Word, but thirsting for God, for the living God. `Worship the Lord in the beauty of holiness'.

2. Be courteous to strangers; shew them the attractiveness of piety and the natural kindness of the Christian. Oblige them with seats and books, and lose no opportunity of encouraging the timid and enquiring. Let none who worship with us have to say, `No man cares for my soul'.

3. If possible, be seated before the time for commencing the service, and attend twice every Sunday.

4. Do not let wet or cold weather, which would not prevent you going to a concert or evening party, prevent you from occupying your usual place in the sanctuary.

5. Bear your own proportion of the Church's burden. If you have the power to contribute, accept no privileges at the expense of another. `Bring an offering and come before Him'.

6. Each member of the Church ought to be doing something for Christ, and render personal aid as far as possible to all the agencies of the Church.

7. Every member absenting himself from the Table of the Lord for six months consecutively, except on account of illness or other satisfactory reasons, forfeits thereby his membership.

8. A Christian Church ought to be composed only of Christian people.

The *minute books* of the church during these years attest the steady rise in church membership with virtually every monthly church meeting approving the reception of new members who were moving into the town from other areas. In 1884 Cooper took over a membership of 293 but by 1903 at the close of his pastorate the church roll stood at 512. This figure included 96 members who provided the nucleus of the St James' Memorial Chapel and 32 who were soon to formally commence the Primrose Hill Church. Cooper faced up to the challenge of growing numbers of children in the Sunday Schools and urged `fellow workers to labour in the vineyard'; as a result the scholars in the three Sunday Schools grew from 1,196 to 1,868 and teachers from 88 to 138 during the same period.

Following the mission of 1889 the Christian Endeavour Society was formed five years later, the beginning of an organisation which was to give the church a willing group of people ready to provide interesting activities and able workers. The young people of the church hired and opened a room in Bristol Street as a shelter from the temptations of the street and a place of Christian contact. This venture closed in 1891 but the demolition of two old cottages in Castle Street provided the site for the erection of a Mission Hall which the young people leased for seven years at £20 per annum. Considerable success followed this initiative. Its young secretary, George Webb, reported at the end of 1894: it has been a year of steady progress all round... a year undoubtedly in which the influence of the Mission has made itself felt in the neighbourhood'. Services were held on Sundays and Thursdays with a Sewing Class on Mondays, a Christian Band on Wednesdays and a `Pleasant Evening for the People' on Saturdays. It even had its own newly purchased organ. Yet another school with 10 teachers and 171 scholars (in 1894) met in the Mission Hall.

A vast range of activities made the life of the church extremely busy. Not only were there the three Sunday Schools but the Doddridge Mutual Improvement Society, the Doddridge Sunday School, the Band of Hope, the School Clothing Club, a Total Abstinence Society, a Branch of the Prayer Union, Christian Endeavour and even a Philip Doddridge Lodge of Good Templars numbering 93 members; this last organisation was initiated by Cooper who was twice Grand Chaplain of Wales and elected grand Chaplain of Northamptonshire in 1893. Cooper was intent on some changes and, as a committed teetotaller, introduced unfermented wine at Holy Communion (a matter which excited differences of opinion). The introduction of chants and anthems, and copper collections from pew to pew (rather than at the door) likewise caused some dissension. The change towards offertory collections began the decline of rented pews, a process which continued until 1924. At the turn of the century the most commodious pews in the prime positions downstairs cost 7 shillings per quarter payable at Christmas, Lady day, Midsummer and Michaelmas; the cheapest pews were one shillings and sixpence, although there were some free pews. Members of the church were encouraged to use tickets when attending Holy Communion, and these tickets were used from time to time when a referendum was needed. On one occasion this method of voting was used when it was proposed to change the sacramental service from afternoons to evenings; members had to write either `afternoon' or `evening' on their tickets. Another vote by ticket was taken when a proposal was made that the congregation should audibly repeat the Lord's Prayer after the pastor; a simple `yes' or `no' was required. It is also amusing to learn that the iron safe in which the church's deeds were to be safely kept resided under the pulpit.

Instructions to the Chapel sexton laid down the details regarding the numerous functions that needed his attendance; in the course of a year he was expected to be on duty for up to seventy-one teas ranging from the Annual Parents' Tea to the Deacons' Tea. For some he received no remuneration but for others he was paid: five shillings each for the Mutual Improvement Society, Senior Class and Young People's teas, half-a-crown for the Choir Supper and Young People's Mission and two shillings for the Ministers and Deacons meeting. In May 1891 a sub-committee recommended:

`That the Caretaker live in close proximity to the Chapel.
That the duties of the caretaker include the following:
The steps leading to chapel galleries and schools, the passages and vestibule to be cleaned and scrubbed every week.
The schools to be cleaned, that is scrubbed, as required but to average not less that 12 times in the year.
The windows to be cleaned by being washed inside and out not less than twice in the year, and to be dusted inside weekly.
The pews to be swept every Monday morning, having first turned the cushions over.
The carpets in pews to be took up once a year, the hassocks and cushions to be beaten in the year.
The cocoa matting in aisles of chapel to be swept and rolled up every week.
The chapel to be dusted on the Saturday, going over it twice.
The W.C's to be thoroughly cleaned and flushed out every week.
The class rooms to be swept and dusted every week, and washed out and scrubbed when required.
The infant class rooms cleaned and scrubbed when dirty, the floor sometimes weekly when weather requires it, and gallery also.
The chapel ventilation to be assisted by opening the windows after morning service when weather not too cold.
The yards swept every week.
The pavement in front of chapel to be swept early on Sunday morning.
The tea urns to be cleaned both inside and outside (outside polished) in the same week in which they have been used, also the tea spoons.
The glassware after being cleaned to be wrapped up separately in paper.
Rooms looked after, gas fires lighted and chairs, tables etc arranged.
Fire and warming apparatus to be attended on Saturdays and early Sunday morning.
Rooms to be arranged for school on Sunday and evening services.
Caretaker to be present at all meetings.
That the remuneration be fixed at the sum of eighteen shillings per week or £46. 16s.0d per annum.
That in addition to the above sum there shall be an additional allowance (to be fixed by scale) for every tea meeting held in connection with the chapel'.

The duties of the sexton were modified as the years passed; extra duties were in the hiring of crockery and linen. The sexton was provided with a tunic and cap, had to be a total abstainer from alcohol and was insured for National Insurance. No room was to be opened (apart from regular meetings) without a permit from the Church Secretary, and twelve hours notice had to be given for the use of rooms and twenty-four if teas were to be provided. Wages rose to sixty pounds a year with rent and rates paid by the church.

The minutes of a deacon's meeting held on 2 December 1891 give a glimpse church life at that time:

'It was stated that Mr & Mrs Stamp accepted the office of caretakers, & Messrs Jeffery & Higgins were requested to see the landlord of a house in Mary's Place, to arrange details of a lease for fourteen years, determinable at the tenants' option at the end of seven years at a weekly rent of five shillings and eight pence. 35 shillings to be allowed the outgoing tenant & 10 shillings to the new caretakers towards defraying cost of removal.
Resolved to accept the offer of Mr Taylor to print 600 manuals for £6.
An arrangement that the pastor could supply Commercial Street pulpit was sanctioned in consequence of the illness of the Rev T. Gasquoine'.

As the century closed a new effort at promoting 'vigorous and progressive Christian work' in the neighbourhood was commenced. The church gave practical help to young people through the Northamptonshire Sunday School Union by helping them find suitable jobs and employers. A Social Improvement Committee set to work in 1899 by acquiring No 46 Horsemarket and converted it into a Working Girls' Club. Although this venture did not succeed, due to the rowdiness of those who attended, it did leave a strong desire to provide week-night activities for girls. This was to materialise in 1916. Work with boys proved more successful with the formation of the 1st Northampton Company of the Boys' Brigade on 19 January 1900. In August that year the boys went to camp at Althorp Park, a favourite venue for Sunday School treats and other outings. With attractions such as cricket, football, club room and band the Boys' Brigade commenced a long and successful history which still continues.

The annual Doddridge Sunday School Treat was something of a *tour de force*. On Thursday 4 July 1901 at 1pm the teachers and scholars of the Doddridge and Mission Hall marched four abreast to Castle Station headed by the Boys' Brigade band. Here they embarked by train for Althorp at 1.30pm followed at 2.10pm by a second train on which were the massed ranks of the St James' End and Primrose Hill scholars and teachers. They, too, had marched to the station four abreast headed by the band. At 3.45pm at Althorp they were all summoned to tea by the sound of a bugle. At 4.30pm games began followed by balloon ascents and parachute descents. A grand parade and review of the Boys' Brigade Company took place at 6pm. Trains returned everyone at 8.15 and 9.15pm. The Sunday School rules demanded that 'All scholars must obtain 25 per cent of the possible marks to be eligible for School Treat. New scholars must regularly attend at least three months before Treat to be entitled to attend same, except by special permission of the Superintendent'. All visitors to the park were also cautioned: 'No donkey riding or driving in donkey carts can be permitted, owing to the disturbance caused to the deer thereby'. A catering list for the 1908 Treat records that 50 lbs sugar, 6lbs tea, 70 loaves of bread, 120 large cakes, 9 gallons of milk and 24lbs of butter were consumed by 400 scholars and 100 teachers & friends.

It was inevitable that the extension of the church into the growing suburban life of the town should require some independent existence. On 21 June 1890 twenty-one signed a letter addressed to the members of the Church at Doddridge, Castle Hill:

'The time has arrived when the Congregations worshipping in our Branch Schools at St James' End and Kingsthorpe Road think that the cause of Christ in those Districts will be better advanced by the appointment of a Minister to the regular work of preaching the Gospel amongst them and the general visitation of the people...we ask the Church to allow us to make the trial for twelve months, of sustaining a joint ministry in our midst - we do not ask or seek any separation at present, from the Parent Church, but believe this course will be for the interest of the cause we all desire namely the spread of the Redeemer's Kingdom amongst men'.

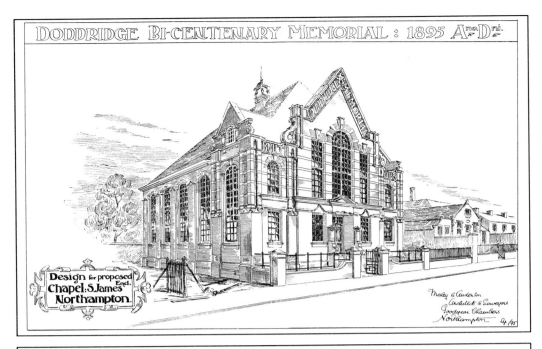

Doddridge Memorial Church 1895

The Castle Hill deacons and the pastor carefully considered the request but thought that 'its adoption would open the way to difficulties which it seems unwise at present to initiate, and therefore recommend that the consideration of the matter be deferred'. But the St James' End branch was virtually independent by 1892 when it elected its own deacons and called the Revd T. Neale of Anstey, Leicestershire to be its pastor. In 1895, in celebration of the bi-centenary of the building of the Meeting House on Castle Hill, ambitious plans were prepared in order to provide both St James End and Kingsthorpe Road branches with new chapels at an estimated cost of £8,500. Thus on 4 March 1896 the seven foundation stones were laid for the Memorial Chapel in St James; the very first service was held on 11 November that year. Built of specially slim facing bricks, Weldon stone and roofed with green slates the Doddridge Bi-centenary Memorial Chapel presented a pleasing appearance to the Main Road. Its formal separation from Castle Hill, however, did not occur until

March 1911. A similar process was in operation at Kingsthorpe Road where the foundation stones for the new Primrose Hill Chapel were laid on 27 December 1901. The official opening of the church took place on 22 January 1903. On 3 June the following year the Revd Frank Burnett became its first pastor and thirty-two members from Castle Hill were 'granted an honourable dismissal' to form its first membership. In departing they expressed a fond farewell:

Primrose Hill Church

'May the God of Peace bless the dear old home - associated with many hallowed memories to those of us who have worshipped there so long - as well as the new home which with the assistance of other brethren has been reared to the honour and glory of the Triune God, at Primrose Hill'.

**Doddridge Chapel, Castle Hill 1889
showing the sundial.**

Doddridge Chapel, Castle Hill 1889.

**Doddridge Chapel, Castle Hill 1894. The new
vestibule. The iron palisade put round the burial
ground (1893/4), formerly used at the front of
All Saints Church, was given by Canon Hull.**

**Doddridge Chapel, Castle Hill 1889. The wall
surrounding the burial ground was removed in
1893/4.**

**Doddridge Chapel
Castle Hill 1894
The new gateway.**

Building developments at Castle Hill itself were also taking place and the southern facade was radically changed. A spacious vestibule was added which, at the time, seemed to some to be like putting a new patch on an old garment. The two canopied doorways disappeared from external view and the old sundial was obscured by the height of the new wall. It was a welcome addition, however, enhancing the warmth of the building in winter and providing a useful gathering space. In 1895 the church resolved to refurbish the entire building as part of its bi-centenary celebrations.

No church consists of a single person but a fellowship of like-minded people worshipping and working together. Castle Hill had gathered to itself men and women of ability who served God faithfully over many years. Between 1878 and 1892 five beloved deacons of the church died, their combined service to the church amounting to one hundred and forty years. As the church gathered for its New Year meeting on 1 January 1896 the minister unveiled a marble tablet placed in the wall near the pulpit to John G. Packe, William Milroy, Pickering Phipps Perry, Jonathan Robinson and James Ellard. The inscription reads:

> *'Gentle in the midst of us as when a nurse cherisheth her own children,*
> *The love that made them serve was the gentleness that made them great*
> *And through the sadness of death these partakers of the grace of Christ*
> *Became the partakers of His glory in the perfect life'.*

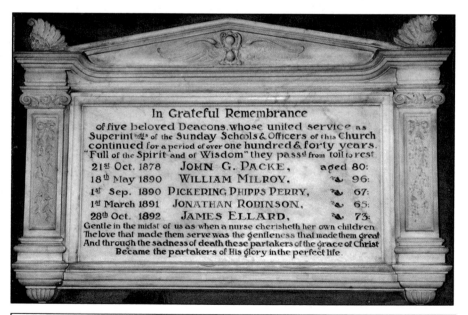

Memorial to 'five beloved Deacons'

On 4 March 1896 one of the church's most faithful friends and diligent workers died; Mrs Pickering Phipps was on that very day expected to lay one of the foundation stones of the Memorial Chapel in St James, with which her name is indissolubly associated. Her death cast a shadow over the event. In January 1897 (as we have already recorded) the church mourned the loss of the Rev Thomas Arnold, its beloved elder statesman and former minister. In November another stalwart died, namely Henry Wilson who was `the leading spirit and guiding hand of the work at Kingsthorpe Hollow' from its early days. Many of the church's leaders were influential in the town and involved in business. Joseph Jeffery, the church treasurer, was elected a Justice of the Peace and was Mayor of the Borough of Northampton in 1899/1900. Names such as Lewis, Webb and Marlow (shoe manufacturers), Trenery (timber merchants), Latimer (corn merchants), Cooper, and Tipplestone (photographers), Adams (bakers) and many others feature constantly throughout the minute books

William Milroy

of the church; generous in their time and substance they provided the backbone of the church's work. William Milroy, who died in 1890 at the age of 96 served the church sixty-one years, many of them as Sunday School superintendent and deacon. The minute book records:

'On Thursday May 22nd his remains were first conveyed to the sanctuary at Castle Hill he loved so well where at 2.30 his funeral service was conducted by the Revs J. Cooper and T. Arnold in the presence of a considerable number of the teachers, members of the Church & other friends. After which, followed by the deacons, superintendents & teachers he was interred in the Cemetery in the grave where the remains of his wife & daughter had previously been deposited'.

In 1895 Castle Hill arranged to affiliate with the Creaton Chapel. The pastors exchanged pulpits once a quarter whilst some of the organisations, such as the choir, made visits to Creaton thus encouraging this village church whose early history was so intertwined with that of Castle Hill. Both churches benefitted from the arrangement. The Revd Spedding Hall and his three deacons at Creaton expressed their gratitude for Castle Hill's *'kind offer of assistance, interest and sympathy with us in the work of Jesus Christ our Lord, which we are trying under somewhat difficult circumstances to carry on here...It will be a strength and a stimulus to us to feel that the burden of our work is shared and lightened...and that our welfare and success are permitted to find, in so large a measure, a warm place in your hearts'* (18/11/1895).

It was at this time (c1897) that great interest was aroused when the original Licence to conduct public worship at Castle Hill in 1695 came into the church's possession. In 1901 the large old clock which was used in the church during the time of Dr Doddridge's ministry was rediscovered. It was bought by Joseph Jeffery and presented to the church. Still more important acquisitions were obtained in 1903 when the Revd Frank Doddridge Humphreys, the last direct descendant of Philip Doddridge allowed them to pass for perpetual preservation into the custody of the Church at Castle Hill. Writing to Cooper from Honiton on 22 May 1903 Humphreys expressed his relief and pleasure in their new home:

'My dear Mr Cooper,

I am forwarding today to your address the 'Doddridge Heirlooms'. Will you express to the Deacons at Doddridge Chapel my feeling of personal indebtedness to them in thus preserving these things from general distribution; others would have valued them for their intrinsic worth, only yourselves and the family for their historic associations. At first the thought of parting with them was a matter of deep regret, not only for the Doctor's sake, but for the sake of the intervening generations who so carefully preserved them, but I feel that these, too, could but rejoice that these things will find their rightful home in the old Sanctuary he loved and cared for. Please accept my thanks for the part which you have taken in this matter.

With kindest regards.
Very sincerely yours
Frank Doddridge Humphreys.

View of the Old Vestry showing the old clock

P.S. The box is not locked, only screwed up. Of the two papers enclosed in this, one is probably the original copy of 'O Happy Day' dictated by the Doctor, and written by his wife; the other, a letter to the Doctor from his sister, the pencilled notes were emendations by my grandfather for the 'Diary & Correspondence'.

The relics include such diverse objects as the cover used on the Communion Table, a first edition of Doddridge's hymns, Mercy Doddridge's court shoes, two Bibles published during the Civil War, a jewel cabinet, 17th century stump work, coats, shirts, purses, gloves, shoe buckles, probate copies of the Doddridge wills, an edition of a rare book written by Sir John Dodderidge, a 17th century pin-cushion and the fragments of a ball dress worn by Mercy Doddridge and given her by the Prince & Princess of Wales. (*Church Manual* 1904 p40). The writings of J. J. Cooper, in co-operation with Thomas Arnold greatly contributed to the recording of the history of the church; their *History of the Church of Doddridge and Reminiscences* published in 1895 plus the articles written for the yearly *Church Manuals* are permanent memorials of the story of the church.

In 1898 the new Nonconformist Marriage Act came into force. This was a welcome change in that it removed from the minister of a Nonconformist place of worship the disability by which he was not allowed, as was an Anglican clergyman, to perform the legal marriage ceremony. Henceforth, like his Anglican brother, he (or any other person authorised for the purpose) could do so without the presence of the registrar. Castle Hill adopted the Act in 1901, and the pastor became the Authorised Person for the performance of marriage.

Cooper took part in the first International Congregational Council held at Boston, U.S.A. in 1899. It made a great impression upon him; he returned with enthusiasm for the Twentieth Century Fund of half a million pounds which was being raised for the furtherance of Congregational ideals. Castle Hill enthusiastically took part and special commemorative meetings were held on 7 November 1900 when the Revd Thomas Gasquoine gave an address on Doddridge's work at Northampton; in the evening a crowded public meeting was held when the memorial tablet to the Revd Thomas Arnold was unveiled by Joseph Jeffery, then Mayor of Northampton, after which the Revd Dr. Guinness Rogers delivered an oration on Philip Doddridge.

The 1902 Education Act provoked Nonconformist agitation. The levying of rates to support the schools of the established church whilst discriminating against Nonconformists produced many 'passive resisters', and Cooper, after weighing up the consequences, decided to oppose the Education Rate. He wrote with passion in his pastor's letter in the *Manual* for 1903:

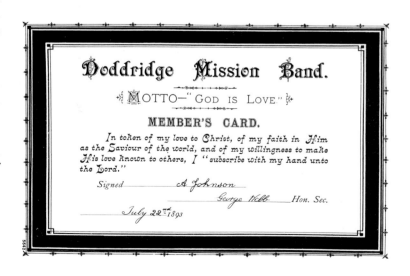

Mission Band certificate

'This New Year brings a crisis in our Free Church life such as we have never faced before. The government Education Bill re-imposes the Church rate for Anglican and Catholic Schools, and the Test Act for the Civil service of teachers, which will shut Nonconformist teachers out of thousands of schools supported by public money. The Bill is so complicated and confusing as to conceal for the present many other unjust provisions...'

He continued by warning that moves were afoot in `extirpating Protestant opinion and practice not only within the Church itself but throughout the land...The Bill provides the machinery to accomplish this'. He was prepared to resist the new rate and, consequently, many of his goods were seized. His successor was to go one step further, being prepared to go to prison rather than pay `for the teaching of error'.

Revd Charles Davie

Henry Cooper

Cooper's health had been giving cause for concern for some time, so in 1901 it was decided to relieve him as much as possible of the burdens of office by appointing an **assistant minister.** This choice fell upon **Charles Davie**, a student at Nottingham Institute. Davie commenced his duties on 2 June 1901. His settlement was doubly welcome as the pastorate at the Memorial Chapel was just then vacant and the supplying of the pulpit there had fallen upon Castle Hill. Davie was ordained to the ministry at an impressive service on 11 June 1903, the charge to the minister being preacher by his college principal, the Revd J. A. Mitchell. At his ordination Davie devoted himself to the pastoral ministry declaring: `The young people are the hope of the church, and it will be my pleasurable duty to take a cordial interest in all that influences the young life of the town'. He married whilst he was at Northampton and his wife was active in supporting him in his work. They soon won their way into the hearts of the people, especially the younger members of the congregation, and Davie remained in warm friendship with Cooper and with the church. The latter's resignation on 21 November left the pastorate vacant, and the way was cleared for Davie to accept the warm invitation of the church at Lower Darwen, Lancashire where he exercised a successful ministry until 1936. He died in 1940.

On 1 May 1902 another notable gathering was held at the church upon the retirement from the presidencey of the Young Men's Bible Class of Mr Henry Cooper F.R.P.S. Henry Cooper had worked devotedly for 35 years with the Bible Class and it had had enormous influence upon many young men. Two hundred former students and friends came to wish him well and thank him for all his devoted labours. He was presented with a rosewood clock, a silver espergne and a revolving bookcase, and messages of gratitude were received from all parts of the country. The oak-lined Cooper Room, previously known as the Green Room, with his photographic portrait is a permanent reminder of his humble devotion to the cause of Christ.

Joseph Cooper's nineteen years of ministry at Castle Hill came to a sudden end. Nearly three years before he had had a heart attack whilst preaching, and this had begun a gradual failing in health. It was hoped that Davie's appointment would provide the essential relief from pastoral responsibility that would lengthen his life, but within two months, on 20 January 1904, Cooper passed away, having just entered his 67th year. His funeral was an occasion of an expression of affection and respect rarely given to anyone in the public eye. H.N Dixon writing of the occasion recorded:

`The procession from the chapel to the cemetery was half a mile in length; the civic authorities and some sixty societies were represented, and the crowds around the grave numbered by thousands. To one whose most obvious characteristic was his retiringness and unwillingness to come into the glare of the footlights this was surely a very remarkable tribute...His ministry had nothing showy about it, but it was aimed at the building up of a true Christian life in the individual, and a true evangelical spirit in the church; and under his pastorate the church life grew not only wider, but perhaps more markedly deeper...Under his ministry the church grew and multiplied...the effect of [his] ministry was to establish a church consciousness that was enduring and permanent'.

His memorial tablet in the church states: `In memory of a Pastor Beloved, the Rev Joseph J. Cooper who after many years of labour in many lands, served this church faithfully as its minister for 19 years until his death, adding to its history, rich in long and happy pastorates, yet another golden page. His was the ministry of the preacher, for he communed less with men than with God: the preacher's voice and the prophet's vision were given him, and he held them as a sacred trust...'

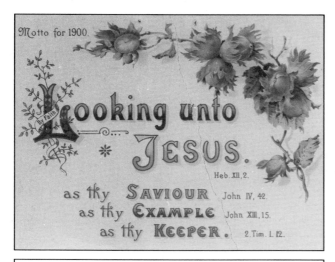

Motto texts for each new year were initiated by Revd J. J. Cooper in 1885.
The motto for 1900 and a new century.

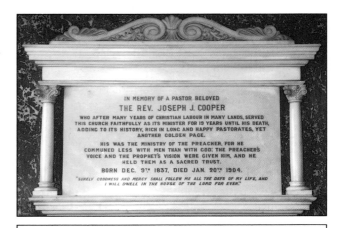

Memorial to Revd Joseph J. Cooper at Castle Hill.

Part 6
1905 - 1930
The ministries of Pierce, Stanley and Evans

Revd William Pierce: 1905 - 1910.

Revd William Pierce

The pastorate, vacant since the close of 1903, was filled early in 1905 by the arrival of the Revd William Pierce. He had been educated in Liverpool and worked as a journalist before entering the Congregational Church from Brecon College in 1879. His first pastoral charge was at Bideford, Devon followed by Leytonstone, Soho Hill in Birmingham, New Court Tollington Park, and also at West Hampstead. He was a cultured and refined preacher who combined a Welsh fervour with imaginative power. Having preached several times during 1904 Pierce had been cordially approached by the church and had accepted the Call. Membership of the church at that time was 456 and had fluctuated between 512 in 1902 and 434 only two years later. Vigorous pruning of the church's membership roll in the latter year by which some seventy names were removed from the roll due to removal from the neighbourhood or having `dropped out of communion with us' accounts for this apparent decrease. Nevertheless, even with the numbers worshipping at St James and Kingsthorpe the overall number of members worshipping at Castle Hill showed an underlying rise; in 1912, after removing those then worshipping at the two other now independent churches, the roll at Castle Hill stood at 282 and rose steadily to 363 by 1920.

Pierce began his ministry with `a trumpet-call to the general body of Church Members, calling them to arms'. There was much to be done, he urged `The Sunday School is wanting several teachers on the boys' side. Help is wanted to form a society for the younger boys and girls to meet from seven to eight on Tuesday evenings. Several tract Distributors are needed to take small districts in the neighbourhood of our Church'. He led a Minister's Catachumen Class and continued the week-night services and grappled with the problem of the morning service which `must be greatly improved before it ceases to be a source of much anxiety'. He was acutely aware of the problems of the immediate environment: `only by unabated zeal and effort can a central church in a poor neighbourhood be maintained whose congregation is scattered over the whole town area'.

He passionately upheld the principles on which Nonconformity stood. His knowledge of the history of Dissent was profound; he claimed for the Dissenting tradition a high place both in the present as well as the past in its witness to Christ as the Supreme Head of the Church and to `the priesthood of all believers'. He was opposed to Erastianism and sacerdotalism. During his ministry in Northampton he wrote and published his masterly treatise *An Historical Introduction to the Marprelate Tracts* which was widely acclaimed. This rich historical sense led him to write and produce the Nonconformist Pageant which was performed to large audiences in the church schoolrooms. It presented dramatic scenes from the local history of Congregationalism; John Penry, Jeremiah Lewis and Philip Doddridge were recreated with a vividness which greatly impressed many of the young people who took part in the pageant. In a series of sermons on *Heroes and Martyrs of the English Reformation* in 1906 Pierce showed his wide knowledge of the development of religious freedom in England. These deeply-held views led him to make a strong stand against the Education Rate. His predecessor had had goods confiscated but Pierce was imprisoned for what he described as 'refusing to pay the Priest's Rate'. On 29 November 1905 he was summoned for the non-payment of fourteen shillings and threepence. A crowd of supporters applauded his stand in the court. He was given three days imprisonment in Northampton Gaol being released on 1 December where a large group of sympathisers waited his return. Some time later he went to prison again as a passive resister, and a third spell in gaol was averted when his deacons paid the rate for him.

The Historic Pageant of Northampton Nonconformity, written by Pierce, attracted large audiences. Mr Higgins and the Misses Chapman, Ward and Nicholls.

Hugh Neville Dixon as Henry Godley

At the annual meeting of the teachers connected with the Doddridge School in 1904 a letter was despatched to the Prime Minister offering congratulations on the satisfactory progress of negotiations following the Dogger Bank Incident and expressing admiration for the peaceable example set by the British Government to the nations of the world. On 14 November the Prime Minister's secretary, Wilfred R. Short replied from 10 Downing Street:

'Mr Balfour desires me to say that he is obliged to you for the congratulations which you have been good enough to convey to him from the annual meeting of the Doddridge Congregational Sunday Schools, Northampton; he has received them with much satisfaction. He hopes that you will take an opportunity of expressing to the members his cordial thanks'.

Pierce commenced the *Doddridge Magazine* in January 1906 as a medium of circulation for church news and the heralding and recording of notable events. In varying forms and under different names the magazine has continued its useful work until the present day. He also founded *The Men's Own* in 1905. This organisation met every Sunday afternoon at ten to three in the church becoming an influential meeting point in the town.

Founded as part of the Brotherhood Movement and impelled by Christian values of friendship and fraternity the Men's Own attempted to reach the unchurched men of the town. Unsectarian and apolitical in object the Sunday afternoon meetings drew a large membership to hear speakers of local and national renown from all walks of life. By 1920 the registered membership had reached five hundred. Whilst the Men's Own did not provide a successful feeder directly to the church it provided a valuable forum for debate and, under successive pastors, developed an organic connection with the church. Things were not always peaceful, and early in its history on 10 May 1907 John Ward, the Labour Party M.P. for Stoke on Trent came to address the meeting. Hecklers from the galleries refused to be quietened in spite of appeals to give Ward a fair hearing. The *Northampton Mercury* reported:

'This proved impossible. Two or three men in each gallery succeeded in raising pandemonium in a meeting of six or seven hundred. At last, the chairman requested Mr Ward to retire to the vestry, as the disturbance was a disgrace to Northampton working men...eventually a persistent hooligan in the gallery on the left of the platform was ejected by willing arms...followed by...the secretary of the local branch of the Social Democratic Federation. During this latter operation Mr Edward Morgan...was injured while assisting. He was conveyed to the hospital where his damaged shoulder was bound up, and then conveyed home. After the disturbers had been removed Mr Ward returned to the platform and gave a short address in which he said that he would return to Northampton in the near future and address a secular meeting where he could deal with rioters in more effective fashion'.

Thankfully few incidents of this nature marred the long history of the Men's Own which survived until the 1980's.

The Mission Hall in Castle Street

1906 saw an outstanding evangelistic mission to the area around the church led by the Revd W.Y.Fullerton of Leicester. Long and careful preparation was made for it and Pierce made it the subject of his pastoral letter and editorial in the church magazine. A number of young people came into the fellowship of the church as a result. During this year the work carried on in the Mission Hall in Castle Street was transferred to the church buildings with great enthusiasm. In the following year the Young Men's Bible Class began a new era under the leadership of Arthur Jones. Two of the newly elected deacons that year were young people. Incandescent gas mantles were added to the chapel thus improving lighting. Death robbed the church in that year of E. H. Dickinson who had been for many years Superintendent of the Sunday School at the Mission Hall.

In 1908 the Revd Thomas Lord of Horncastle who had reached the age of one hundred was invited to preach at the Harvest festival services; Lord had been converted to Christianity at Castle Hill and had joined the church in 1836. Sadly he died before he could fulfil his engagement. It was in this year that the church launched into publishing; edited by Mrs G. Jeffery *The Northampton Cookery Book* contained recipes contributed by some 130 people. It became very popular and successful. Intriguing recipes ranged from *Buffalo Bill Pudding* to *A Cure for a relaxed throat*. The well-known Christian writer from Northampton, Marianne Farningham Hearne, penned the following poem as an introduction:

So long as we must eat to live,
Let everyone true honour give
To British matron, and to maid,
For we, who revel unafraid
In tasty dishes here displayed
Serenely con these pages over
And always new delights discover.
With such things nicely boiled or browned,
E'en Doddridge would no fault have found,
And all the worthies since his days
Would eat, enjoy, and whisper praise.
For breakfasts, dinners, suppers, teas,
Here are the dainties sure to please.
So, readers, pray be sweet as honey,
And help the old church with your money.

1909 saw the advent of lantern preaching services and the presentation to George Higgins of an illuminated address on his 25 years as Sunday School superintendent. In the following year the Sunday School celebrated its centenary in style as a thanksgiving for the earnest labour and steady faithful toil of the teachers and officers. The Mayor and Corporation attended the morning service on 10 September, and in the afternoon the six Sunday Schools united to fill the church where they were addressed by Sir Joseph Compton Rickett M.P. Other gatherings followed in the succeeding week with the Revd Carey Bonner attending. One veteran, namely William Evans, was unable to be present due to his advanced age; it is said that he had sat under seven pastors and had survived!

The Doddridge (Castle Hill) Church and Sunday School choirs were formed in 1908 and swept the board at the Northamptonshire Musical Competitions in April 1909. The *Echo* reported (26.4.1909):

'The School Choir, which had been formed just a year, carried off premier honours against the choirs from the local day schools in the two part competition on Friday. On Saturday the Church followed up this success by winning the beautiful challenge banner for sight reading in an unusually keen contest, being awarded 19 marks out of a possible 20. Both choirs came in for heartiest

---

Household Quantities.

FAIR AVERAGE PER HEAD PER WEEK.

¼-lb Tea.   Equal to 28 teaspoonfuls.

¼-lb. Coffee.

¼-lb. Cocoa.

3½ to 7lb. Meat.   Usual quantity, 5-lb.

½-lb. Butter.

½-lb. Cheese.

1-lb. Bacon.

3½-lb. Potatoes (about)

7-lb. Bread.

½-lb. Soap.

1-quart Milk.   One third of a pint usual consumption for an adult daily (not for children).

Bedroom Candles, 8 to lb.; Ordinary time for burning, 4½ hours.

Bundles of Wood, 25 for 1/-   Each bundle should light three fires, or two kitchen fires.

Gas from 15/- to 18/- yearly, with a good burner.

Coal.   1 ton a month for kitchen range is ample.

Title page of the church's Cookery Book

MR. JOSEPH JEFFERY, J.P.
Deacon 1891—1927.
Church Treasurer 1891—1919.

MR. GEORGE HIGGINS.
S.S. Superintendent 1883—1919.
Deacon 1891—1927,
Church Secretary 1901—1927.

MR. W. G. WARD.
Deacon 1917—1927.

Joseph Jeffery J.P., George Higgins & W. G. Ward.

congratulations yesterday. They were trained by Mr Handel Hall (organist), who had the additional satisfaction of hearing his son secure first prize in the junior pianoforte section of 40 competitors'.

1910 saw the wiping out of the bi-centenary debt which had been spread over a term of fifteen years; true to the ways of Congregationalism the clearing of this debt was thought to be fitly celebrated by the inauguration of a new Renovation Fund amounting to some £300. It was a year during which Pierce concluded his pastorate as he was called to be the minister at Higham's Park in Essex. On 9 October he preached his farewell sermons, the church bidding him and his wife a fond farewell. At the same service Miss Louisa Robinson for another term of service as an overseas missionary in India.

Pierce left the church in a strong position with a total of 433 members, 269 at Castle Hill, 152 at St James (in the following year to be officially recognised as an independent church), and 12 non-resident in Northampton. The breadth of activities in the church is reflected in the *Manual* for that year with the Sunday School (Secretary John Archer), Choir (Fred Cater), Sunday School Choir (W. Handel hall), Christian Endeavour Society (J.Knight & A. Gray), Young Men's Senior Class (Arthur Jones), Young People's Institute (W.Kinch), Gymnasium (Chas. Macquire), Doddridge Men's Own (R.W.Cass & F.Harrison), London Missionary Society Auxiliary (Mrs H.N.Dixon), Band of Hope (F.Hornsey), Free Church Council Parochial Scheme (S.B.Wilson), L.M.S. Watchers' Band (Mrs George Higgins), Boys' Brigade (T.L.Burrows), Maternal Meeting (Mrs George Jeffery), Junior Children's Service (Walter Kinch and F.Godfrey), Young Ladies' Working Party (Mrs John Archer), Clothing Club (Malcolm Nash), Mothers' Meeting (Mrs George Higgins), and Female Bible Mission (Miss A. Chapman). The church took seriously its responsibilities to the wider Christian community with representatives to the County Congregational Association, the Congregational Union and the Northampton & District Free Church Council.

The life of churches throughout the world had been deeply stirred by the 1910 World Missionary Conference held at Edinburgh. In order to bring the conference's message home to local church life a series of meetings was held at Castle Hill; the aim was to guide the stream of enthusiasm awakened at Edinburgh into practical and lasting channels. On 4 April Dr Horton, Mr Vanner Early and the Revd E.P.Powell all spoke to a crowded public meeting, quickening the missionary spirit in the churches of Northampton.

Revd R. Morton Stanley

Revd R. Morton Stanley M.A., B.D. 1911 - 1917

The church took an unprecedented step in inviting a student from college to be the next minister to take sole pastoral charge. R. Morton Stanley was senior student at Yorkshire United College; although he had no pastoral experience he had worked in business before entering college and had had the widened training of university life at Edinburgh. He had also benefitted from the influence of Dr Burford Hooke who led the college missionary society. Stanley brought the gifts of a well-trained intellect, youthful enthusiasm, and a friendly affectionate disposition. The church showed itself remarkably united and warm in its Call which was sent on 28 May 1911. After a short while Stanley replied, accepting the invitation, and his ministry commenced on 9 July. He was ordained at a solemn and impressive service on 14 September. His college principal, the Revd Griffiths Jones D.D. together with Professor Armitage, Dr Burford Hooke, the Revd William Pierce and others took part.

Stanley's ministry commenced with enthusiasm, some fifty new members joining the church in the first two years of his ministry. He threw himself heart and soul into all aspects of the church's life including the Men's Own which continued to prosper. As pastor-elect he conducted the Coronation Services on 18 June 1911 in recognition of the coronations of King George V and Queen Mary on the 22nd. His photograph appears in the service sheet with a youthful face and shock of hair. In 1912 he was married to Miss Mabel Moore at Oakengates, Shropshire; this happy event was celebrated over the next few months at Castle Hill with a summer garden party when Mrs Stanley was introduced to the church members and a wedding gift presented. Later in September the minister and his wife held an *At Home* reception in the schoolroom.

The formation of the Women's Own in the autumn of 1912 gave a new opportunity of work among the women of the neighbourhood. Founded on similar lines as the Men's Own, with no restrictions on denominational lines, the new organisation 'attempted to provide an elevating influence among the womanhood from the industrial homes around the church, to give by the meetings a relief from the monotony and drudgery of home life, and over and above this to come into closer touch and personal sympathy with their lives'(HND). Handbills were distributed to nearly every house in the town, and the first meeting attracted an audience of 600. So began another organisation that was to thrive for many years. In February 1913 the minister conducted a four day mission aimed at attracting young people. As a result some twenty young people became more committed to the Christian fellowship of the church.

Life continued at Castle Hill with an unusual Veteran's Tea in March 1912; all members of the church of 35 or more years standing were the guests and all but five of the twenty-six invited were able to attend. Another veteran, namely the organ, fell into senile decay. Determined to face the problem the church decided to install another instrument. Andrew Carnegie sent a handsome donation of £350 towards the cost, estimated to be £850. The choir undertook to spearhead the fund-raising needed. The new Compton organ was opened and dedicated on Thursday 2 October 1913 by two organ recitals by F. Heddon Bond who had supervised its erection. It was used for the first time in public worship on the following Sunday when the Mayor and Corporation attended in state. The total cost, including the necessary alterations in seating amounted to practically one thousand pounds. The *Echo* reported (29.9.1913):

'The organ erected in Doddridge (Castle Hill) Church, Northampton...contains many features of unusual interest to musical folk, indeed the whole scheme is so out of the ordinary as to have evoked considerable discussion among local organists...In point or size, judged by the number of organ stops, the organ ranks among the largest in the county...There are three manuals and a complete compass of pedals...The instrument is placed on either side of the galleries at the pulpit end of the church, and very much improves the appearance of the building. It is enclosed in handsome cases of selected dark Austrian oak...They have been designed to harmonise with the style of the entablature at the pulpit end of the chapel and present a fine bold appearance. The front is partially rounded and the silvered organ pipes supported by [a] 12-inch moulded cornice...The console of oak is placed immediately in front of the pulpit. It is beautifully fitted, and the stop knobs are of solid ivory. At the console is an automatic starter for the electro-motor which drives the blowing apparatus and generates a low-voltage current for the action work. The console is connected to the pipework by an electro-pneumatic cable'.

The church thus acquired one of the most advanced organs of the day replacing the organ situated in the gallery over the entrance to the church; this instrument had been purchased second-hand for £191 in 1875 from Stapleton Parish Church, Gloucestershire and enlarged in 1891. It was sold to the Baptist Chapel in Measham, Leicestershire. The earliest record of an organ at Castle Hill goes back to 1850; this particular instrument proved unsatisfactory for the enlarged building and was subsequently sold for £50 in 1875.

Organ recitals, October 1913

1914 began quietly and Stanley looked forward in his New Year pastoral letter looked forward to a fruitful year of activity. At the July church meeting good wishes were conveyed to the church at Elberfeld, and even in August the magazine was wishing everyone a happy refreshing holiday. But even before the magazine was in the hands of its readers a devastating war had commenced. Events followed one another in shocking sequence. Young men began to enlist and within a month the school buildings were commandeered for military use. Although this did not last long it was a sinister reminder of what the war was going to mean. Within another month a flood of Belgian refugees poured over the Channel to England. The Castle Hill people were among the first to volunteer help, and two families, comprising fourteen people of three generations, were received, housing was found for them, furniture and money given, and help to provide their own earnings. During their time with the Castle Hill people three babies were born and two of the older refugees passed away. One family dispersed after a time, some of them returning to Antwerp. The other family stayed until the close of the war in 1918. H. N. Dixon, who was mainly responsible for these unfortunate families, wrote: 'The sympathy evoked by the necessities of these outcasts from home and country, and the deep personal interest taken in their welfare by many of the people of the church made a bright spot in the prevailing darkness'.

The problems of war pressed acutely upon the younger ministers. Some felt that they should not shelter behind their holy orders thus avoiding active service. Stanley felt keenly that he should be actively engaged in the defence of his country and in fighting a righteous cause. Yet if ever there were needed the preaching of the Gospel at home then this was the time; his church needed his guidance and support especially as the list of casualties was mounting. He reluctantly passed by opportunities for enlistment, and whilst the church would have not stood in his way there was great relief that he stayed in Northampton.

Church life had to continue. In 1915 Mrs Jonathan Robinson died, a deaconess since 1892 and an indefatigable worker for the church. Numerous organ recitals were held since the installation of the new organ; one outstanding recital was given by Professor Firmin Swinnen, the organist of Antwerp Cathedral and Belgium's foremost musician. Funds were raised for the support of the Belgian refugees eighty of whom attended the recital. During the same year the Christian Endeavour Society attained its 21st birthday and a special service and tea were held to celebrate the occasion. But war continued to cast its shadows. By the end of the year some 77 names had been listed on the Roll of Honour. The home end was being organised to keep in touch with those in the trenches and battlefields. Miss Alice Chapman undertook the task of being church correspondent and parcels were sent that Christmas to those on `the far flung battle line'.

1st Company Northampton Boys' Brigade, Castle Hill. 1915.

War dominated the pages of the *Church Manual* for 1916, thinning the pages down and dominating directly or indirectly all that was reported. Yet in the midst of the gloom one bright spark suddenly kindled. On 27 March a Girls' Life Brigade was formed under the captaincy of Miss W. Wilkes. Miss Louisa Robinson returned that year after 27 years service as a missionary in India and was welcomed back at a special meeting in June. Messrs Joseph Jeffery and George Higgins were elected life deacons, and the responsibility for the Belgian refugees passed from the church to the town committee although the friendships made were continued. Again and again the war took its heavy toll. One of the losses most severely felt was the death of Beavan Pitt, Lieutenant in the Airforce, who had been Assistant Secretary of the Sunday School and one of the most promising younger men of the church.

In July 1917 Stanley marked the occasion of his sixth anniversary as pastor, yet three months later had received a unanimous invitation to be the minister of the church at Newlands, Lincoln. It was a pressing call and Stanley agonised over his decision. After much thought and discussion he accepted the Call and bade farewell to Castle Hill at a crowded meeting on 22 November. The church deeply regretted his departure and representatives of many churches in the town came to bid him God speed.

Miss Alice Chapman, church correspondent to the `boys' in the trenches, 1914 -18.

Revd J. E. Evans B.A. 1918 - 1930

Revd John E. Evans

Fortunately, the pastoral vacancy only lasted for six months. A visit from the Revd J. E. Evans of Trinity Church, Bridlington in March 1918 was quickly followed by another in April and his acceptance of the church's Call on 12 May. However, difficulties became apparent when a new Military Service Bill was brought before Parliament intimating at the conscription of ministers. German advances were making the government very nervous. The deacons discussed the matter with the prospective minister, but relief was apparent when the idea of ministerial conscription was dropped. The church was free to appoint, and Evans took up his duties on 4 July.

Evans brought with him a youthfulness tempered by experience. As a Leader in the front line of Huts for the Y.M.C.A. in 1916/17 was to stand him in good stead when the men on service began to arrive home. The recognition services for the new minister were crowded and enthusiastic with Dr A.E.Garvie, Revd Morton Stanley, the Rector of St Peter's Northampton, the Mayor (Cllr. A.J.Chown) and others taking part. Evans threw himself at once into the activities of the church which soon began to respond to his interest and help. During that autumn Mr W. Handel Hall was presented with an illuminated address and a clock in recognition of 25 years as organist. But all activity paled into insignificance when Armistice day was declared on 11 November. The walls of the old Meeting House had seen many gatherings but none to compare for depth of feeling and solemn emotion with the great Thanksgiving Service held on the 13th. Evans conducted the service during which he preached on Isaiah 40, `Cry unto her that her warfare is accomplished'. Music included the *Te Deum* and concluded with Handel's *Hallelujah Chorus.*

The New Year of 1919 began with an immense sense of relief that the war had ended, yet many problems were encountered in its aftermath. The task of reconstruction in political and social life was enormous, and the ravages upon religious life were equally profound. The piecemeal process of demobilisation made it impossible for the church to give a general welcome to the returning troops; it had to be done in relays. The first *Welcome Home* social was held on 7 February when some fifty demobilised men were honoured. Other similar events were held later in the year. On 28 July the Northampton Battalion of the Boys' Brigade held a Memorial Service at Castle Hill. The crowded church included the Mayor and Mayoress, the former mayor and other dignitaries. The battalion colours were carried into the church, received by the minister and placed in front of the pulpit. A powerful sermon on the victory of life over death stirred many in the Brigade to live lives worthy of the sacrifices that had been made. At the close the congregation stood with bowed heads while outside the building buglers sounded the *Last Post* and *Reveil99le.*

The cramped premises in which the whole week-day and Sunday work of the church had to operate put great difficulties in extending the scope of the Boys' Brigade and other youth activities as well as the Men's Own. Ideas were put forward by the deacons as to the possibility of improving the premises as a War Memorial, even to the extent of pulling down all the old buildings (except the chapel itself) and erecting new ones. After much deliberation and the presentation of many plans it was reluctantly concluded that with the limited ground available the only adequate scheme would be far too expensive.

A. E. Hodge

John Archer

An innovation in 1919 was the introduction of the May Festival as part of the Sunday School's activities. Great efforts were made in its preparation and by far the largest audiences attended since the pageant of 1910. A Floral Festival was followed by the Coronation of the May Queen. During 1919 the Primary Department of the Sunday School was established under the leadership of Miss Nellie Ward. A Missionary Pageant was arranged by Miss Robinson depicting scenes in the life of Chundra Lela, a persecuted Indian Christian; this helped to stimulate interest in the London Missionary Society. After forty years of service to the Sunday School George Higgins retired on account of increasing ill-health. Arthur Hodge and John Archer were elected co-superintendents in his place. On 30 July a portrait of Mr Higgins and a silver candelabra were presented to him and his wife. During the year the Guild of Fellowship and Service was founded under the guidance of A. E. Rodhouse; the object was for young men to meet together to study the principles and practice of Christian service. The Christian endeavour celebrated its first quarter century. Joseph Jeffery retired after thirty years as Church Treasurer, with J. P. Robinson elected in his place. At the Church A.G.M. in January suitable recognition of Joseph Jeffery's service to the church was made in the presentation of a testimonial. Recognition, too, was given for the work of Mrs Jeffery and Miss Daisy Jeffery who had assisted her father in his treasurer's duties.

A new order of Moderators in Congregationalism came into being in 1919; the Revd H.H.Carlisle M.A. of Balham was appointed to the East Midlands Province in which Northampton is situated. He soon took opportunity to visit Castle Hill and became a welcome visitor. The wider orbit of Congregationalism impinged upon the church in 1920 with the Missionary Exhibition and Pageant held during may in the Town Hall. Castle Hill folk enthusiastically supported this venture. The Third International Congregational Council was held in Boston U.S.A and Castle Hill was represented by Mr & Mrs Rodhouse. The tercentenary of the sailing of the Mayflower commemorated a vital epoch in Congregationalism. In Northampton a series of meetings was held culminating in a Mayflower pageant which was held at the Town Hall under the direct of Laurie Toseland.

The unveiling of the War Memorial in the vestibule of the church was undoubtedly the most notable event in the outward life of the church in 1920. It took place on 4 July. In a simple and reverent ceremony led by the minister the Mayor, F.W.Kilby, performed the act of unveiling. Placed in the centre of the interior wall of the vestibule filling the space between the two doors, the memorial consists of three panels in oak relieved with carved cappings and pilasters. The large centre panel covers the space between the two windows and is flanked on each side by a narrow panel. The centre panel states: `In honoured memory of the men of this Church who laid down their lives in the Great War, 1914 - 1918'. It also contains the names of the men who were killed and their regiments, in two columns divided by a carved flaming Greek torch symbolising the handing-on of their sacrifice as a trust to be passed on to the generations to come. At the bottom of the panel is the verse: `Their name liveth for evermore'. The left panel contains a carved and gilded cross relieved with a

Dedication of the War Memorial, July 1920

laurel wreath denoting the sacrificial nature of their death and the prize of glory won by that sacrifice. The text reads: `Whosoever will lose his life for My sake shall find it'. The right panel contains a Crusader's shield on which is placed a gilded cross and above, an emblazoned crown. The text reads: `Be thou faithful unto death, and I will give thee the crown of life'.

The overall desire was not just to commemorate the war dead but to should look to the future. The renovation of the buildings, a long-needed task, was put into operation in 1920 to fittingly mark the 225th anniversary of the building of the chapel. A series of meetings and services marked the event during which some of the great preachers of the day gave their message from the Castle Hill pulpit. A Mission of Consecration, the introduction of the new *Congregational Hymnary*, the revival of Sunday evening services for children, and the coming of age of the Boys' Brigade were important features of an eventful year. Writing at the time H.N.Dixon recorded:

`And so the year ended, with a bright and hopeful outlook for the church. Its institutions were in full swing, its accommodation taxed to overflowing on every night of the week; the finances healthy if not affluent; and a spirit of warmth and loyalty to the church and its pastor pervaded the community. The membership had increased from 333 in 1918 to 358 at the close of 1920, in spite of a somewhat drastic revision of the church roll in the meantime, by which 19 members of doubtful standing were removed from the roll; and after a number of years of constant and disconcerting decrease in the number of Sunday School scholars, the numbers began again to show a small but steady growth'.

Evans engaged with the problems of the times. In November 1921 he preached against the secularisation of Sunday. The world, he argued was waging a war against the Sabbath, and a weekly day of rest was laid down by the recent Peace Treaty. *`What is the Sabbath to many? A day for motor trips, for golf, tennis, drinking, for mere pleasure or lolling about? The Sabbath is a precious heritage, an immeasurable agency in carrying mankind forward to its divine destiny'.* In other sermons he sought to show that the Christian spirit was not opposed to good business or honourable sporting activities. Christians were not kill-joys but everything had to be put into a proper perspective. At the 1923 A.G.M. he addressed the pressing issues of the day. Admitting that Christianity did not have the hold on people's lives that it once had he made reference to the materialism, class selfishness and `lessened sanctity of home life and the marriage tie'. He stressed that the Gospel was the sole key to the world's ills and pleaded for a deeper devotion to the ideals and life of the church. Referring to the smallness of the morning congregation he said that one of the reasons was the lack of a tram service on Sunday mornings. Such difficulties, he challenged, were a test of Christian loyalty, and `easy religion made flabby souls'. Evans was certainly registering the very different social milieu that had developed since the turn of the century; the war years had deepened a sense of disillusionment and social dislocation. Castle Hill itself was increasingly realising that is was a down-town church with much of its support reliant on transport from the suburbs. The documents of the period stress the efforts made to maintain and strengthen the church's witness in a changing society.

The Boys' Brigade Handbell Ringers performed at the B.B. Rally & Demonstration at the Albert Hall, London in April 1915. The handbells were a gift to the company from George Webb.

As General Secretary of the Congregational Union of England and Wales Mr Evans was influential in bringing its 81st Autumnal Assembly to Northampton between 1st and 5th October 1923. It was a major event drawing a huge number of delegates from every part of England and Wales. Organisation was thorough and detailed with all six Congregational churches in the town cooperating. The assembly commenced with a reception at the Town Hall hosted by the Mayor, Ald. Charles Earl J.P. and chaired by Sir Ryland Adkins. A vast array of meetings and services took place, many centering on Castle Hill as the mother church of Congregationalism. A united mass meeting for children at the Exchange Cinema, a Liberation Society Breakfast, colleges' reunion meetings, public meetings, conferences on many aspects of Congregationalism and youth rallies made for a full timetable. Events spilled out from Northampton to Wellingborough, Market Harborough, Kettering, Long Buckby, Rothwell and Desborough. As part of the Assembly a memorial to Robert Browne, the 'Father of Congregationalism' was unveiled in St Giles churchyard where his remains lie. The Autumnal Assembly left a stunning impression on all who were involved; Northampton had never seen the like before.

The fifth annual May Festival in 1923 culminated in an operetta entitled Lollipopland and performed
by the Sunday School. It was directed by Laurie Toseland, Dennis Hall led a string band,
Nellie Ward presided at the piano and Phyllis Preston was crowned May Queen.

Another May Festival in the early twenties
The May Queen is possibly Nellie Bisecker

The Castle Hill A.G.M. in January 1924 heard the encouraging report: 'A pleasing feature of Doddridge is its successful activities among the young people. Our premises throb with life every night of the week. We are rich in leaders, and to them we give our sincere thanks'. In the following year the minister and deacons entertained to supper all church workers at Castle Hill in recognition of all their services. Some 150 enjoyed a social evening during which Evans encouraged them to double the membership of the church; he indicated that special missions were being planned and that he would preach the Sunday School lesson for the following Sunday at every evening service. Clearly there were underlying concerns over changing attitudes in society. In 1927 national statistics showed that 243,000 fewer scholars were attending Baptist, Congregationalist and Wesleyan Sunday Schools. Even at Castle Hill, which had hitherto escaped serious decline, a loss of 43 scholars was

The Merrie England Bazaar, held at the Town hall in February 1925 transformed the entire hall into a medieval village with stall holders in authentic costume. It was opened on its first day by Lady Knightley of Fawsley and on the second by George Bull Esq. of Wellingborough. Over £1000 was raised for church funds.

Visit of the Bishop of Peterborough to Castle Hill

reported. John Archer, acting Secretary of the church expressed his disappointment at the figures and remarked that a down-town church should not be regarded as `down and out'. The Revd Harold Bickley, addressing a conference at Castle Hill entitled *The Crisis and the Opportunity* spoke of the decline of religion in the home as the major factor in Sunday School decline. It was not, he declared a result of the war, because decline was seen in 1906 when church membership had reached an all-time record. The advent of the motor car aided the decline of Sunday as a church-going day. He congratulated Castle Hill on its vigorous programme to attract young people. Ever alert to new possibilities for young people the church had commenced a Girl Guide company in 1922 together with a Brownie Pack.

In every way the church was attempting to maintain its high standards and was coping very well. It had played its part in the raising of half a million pounds for the Congregational Forward Movement which had completed its task at the end of 1925. The church was one of the few churches able to meet its financial obligations without recourse to annual sales of work and other fund-raising activities. It was in this year that the accounts books cease showing income from pew rents; for more than two decades the money raised from *collections* had increased with a steady decline in income from pew rents. The Bazaar held in 1925 raised a remarkable sum and it was proudly announced that it was only the third such event ever held by the church in all its 250 years of history; each succeeding bazaar had doubled its predecessor's efforts, £318 in 1900, £520 in 1905, and the 1925 *Merrie England Bazaar* £1021. It was reported that there were `many smiling faces' at Castle Hill.

In 1926 new premises in Castle Street were presented to the church by Mr & Mrs H. N. Dixon. Previously used as a mission hall by the church and latterly by St Katharine's Church they were to be used to accommodate Castle Hill Sunday School scholars, meetings and other purposes. The building had been thoroughly redecorated and renovated. The opening ceremony was hampered by heavy rain so the ceremonial door opening was dispensed with. During 1926 the Bishop of Peterborough was welcomed to Castle Hill by the minister and deacons, an historic occasion which recalled the times some two centuries before when Philip Doddridge had a cordial working relationship with many Anglican bishops including the Archbishop of Canterbury.

Bryn Evans

Sadly, tragedy was to strike the Evans family in 1925 when their only child, Bryn Davies Evans aged 15, unexpectedly died following an operation. The family were spending a holiday at Wrexham when the tragedy occurred. Bryn had been a promising student at the Town & County School, and had been a member of a party from the school's Officer Training Corps which had visited Belgium and had met the King. He had been admitted a member of the church only a few months previously. The large brass cross on the organ console was dedicated to his memory. On returning to Northampton his father still preached to his congregations on the following Sunday.

From 16 to 23 March 1930 the church mounted a spectacular celebration of the Bi-centenary of the Ordination and Ministry of Philip Doddridge. The living descendant of Doddridge, the Revd Frank Doddridge Humphreys of Lavenham, Suffolk led the opening services. A Public Luncheon at the Wedgewood Cafe in Abington Street, a Public Tea in the Doddridge Schoolroom, a Public Meeting led by Revd Arthur Pringle, plus a Pageant of Doddridge's life written and produced by Laurie Toseland made for a memorable celebration.

Evans ministered at Castle Hill for twelve years during which time he became active as secretary of the Northamptonshire Congregational Association for ten years, and President in 1929-30, President and Secretary of the Northampton free Church Council, President of the County Federation of Free Church Councils, President of the Northampton Christian Endeavour Federation, President of the Northampton Men's Own (his wife was president of the Women's Own), the President of the Cymric Society which he had helped to reinstate in the town, and a member of the Congregational Union of England and Wales. He was a strong supporter of the Bethany Homestead which was commenced by generous co-operative effort by the Baptist and Congregationalist churches of the town. The first foundation stones were laid in 1925 and the first homes opened in June 1926. He was also instrumental in formulating *The Citizen's Friend* as a bureau of information upon problems of daily living.

A civic service concluded the Bicentenary of Philip Doddridge's Ordination. March 1930.
In the procession are the mayor (Cllr Ralph Smith), Miss Bouverie and
Sir Charles Knightley (Hospital Grand Visitor) and other dignitaries.

Evans announced in May 1930 that he had accepted the Call to the pastorate of the Harlesden Congregational Church, London. He had served Castle Hill faithfully for twelve years, maintaining peace and advancing its fellowship life; he had been in the ministry for twenty-five. At his final services he bade farewell:

'You and I look with hope to the future. I have sought to preach a strenuous gospel. I have tried to preach it in the light of modern learning, while still maintaining loyalty to the christ of our Father. My ministry has been more of a teaching ministry than sensational, because I have thought more of its permanent value than of its temporary impressiveness. It has been my endeavour to bring the comfort of an understanding heaven to the needs and experience of your everyday life. I have sought to keep the ideal high, so I can rest in faith for the seed to fructify, and shall be thankful if the past shall have prepared for a nobler future'.

Mrs Evans left a lasting memorial in the form of the Women's Own. She humorously commented that when she went to Harlesden she would need all her diplomatic skills. The Castle Hill diaconate, all men, had given her good practice in careful handling: 'The Doddridge deacons and leaders I know and can attribute to each a certain quality they represent, and speak to them accordingly. To some I can make a joke and they enjoy it. To others I have to be very serious. They would take a joke as an offence. So I shall have to be very careful in Harlesden for a start, or I shall be making jokes to the wrong people and offending them for life'. There is no doubt that she continued working in harmony with the new congregation as she had done in Northampton.

Part 7
1930 - 1963
The ministries of Edmondson and Wallace.
Commercial Street Congregational Church.

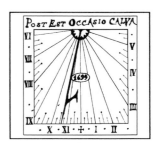

Revd John W. Edmondson 1931 - 1951

Revd John Edmondson

The church soon set about the task of finding a new pastor, and before the end of the year had invited the Revd John W. Edmondson of Park Congregational Church, Camden to accept the pastorate. He preached during November and accepted the Call. He opened his ministry on 26 January 1931 preaching a sermon that morning warning of the dangers of trying to fan the flames of revival without having the patience to wait for spiritual growth. He was alluding to the contemporary campaign by the Congregational Union which aimed at general revival: *'The old story that God created the world in a hurry - six days was enough - that he created man with a word, sounds very wonderful. But it is by no means so wonderful as the revelation of modern science, which shows God had worked for millions of years creating the conditions under which man could come into being, and took milleniums making man'.*

Edmondson had been assistant at Trinity Church, Peterborough in 1914 having pastoral oversight at Glinton. He had cycled forty miles to Castle Hill on one occasion to attend a County Association meeting. He had been encouraged into the ministry by the Revd Matson and had been trained at the Yorkshire United College before taking on his first pastorate at Peckham. He had been minister at Camden for the past five years. The *Northampton Congregationalist* (Dec. 1931) described him as *'a minister of strong personality, eager and sympathetic, a good preacher, and a hard worker who knows pretty well all there is to know about the organisation of young people's interests and work. Mr Edmondson may rely on a hearty welcome upon his return to this county, and we know we are expressing the sentiments of every Northampton Congregationalist in adding the wish that under his vigorous leadership the old Church on Castle Hill may continue to occupy the prominent position in the religious and civic life of the town and county that it has so long and worthily maintained'.* Among the many dignitaries welcoming him the Rector of St Peter's attested the cordial relationship between his church and Castle Hill.

The church community that Edmondson began to serve in 1931 numbered 367 members, just one less than the previous year. Finances were adequate although no cause for complacency; income from all sources, reported

Men's Own Sportsmen's Service, Sunday 8 December 1929. Guest speaker was Lord Burghley (6th from left), the winner of the quarter mile hurdle race at the 1928 Amsterdam Olympic Games.

W. G. Oram the treasurer, amounted to over £25 per week. Twenty-five organisations within the church were active and served both church and community. The New Year's message by the Dean of Canterbury, broadcast on the B.B.C. was followed by the sounds of Doddridge's hymn 'O God of Bethel'.

One of the new minister's interests was the Workers' Educational Association. As a student pastor he had helped to organise W.E.A classes in the West Riding. He thus began a young men's class in biology at Castle Hill. Deeply interested in the League of Nations he always encouraged interest in its ideals. He began redeveloping the Sunday School at Castle Hill, forming a Senior Department under the leadership of John Archer and commencing a Beginner's Department. He produced a weekly printed leaflet of the church's services and activities. Of the former, details of the hymns, readings, sermon subjects were given. Believing that as the Free Churches have a right to take the best from all denominations he adopted responses from the Prayer Book and used Anglican Collects for the Day. The *Chronicle & Echo* reported: '*...they try to have fellowship with the Established Church by reading the Collect for the day. Then they have borrowed from the Quakers by having periods of silent prayer. At Doddridge too the new style of chanting, introduced by Dr Robert Bridges, is used. Altogether, the service here is both novel and beautiful. It has both restfulness and sincerity and, above all, reverence'.*

Sadly, not all saw the innovations in a tolerant light and Edmondson came in for sharp criticism in the press. *'Whether a recent innovation or not'*, wrote one critic, *'the fact that members of a Nonconformist Chapel should sit down and solemnly decide without rhyme or reason to lift bodily and make use of certain portions of the Prayer Book strikes me as very curious; indeed, a Churchman has told me that it borders on impudence...It seems strange to me ...imitating a form of service deliberately rejected over 200 years ago by the founders of the Free Churches...One reason why the Church as a whole is losing ground today is its slavish adherence to obsolete notions and religious jargon the present generation totally fails to understand...That the traditions of Dr Doddridge will be maintained at Doddridge Church is the hope of CONGREGATIONALIST'.* Edmondson was not deflected by such criticism and succeeded in developing a distinctive style of worship at Castle Hill which has influenced worship practice to the present day.

Many activities continued throughout the thirties. In 1931 the organ was officially reopened after further improvements. Two years later a party from Castle Hill travelled to Tewkesbury and Upton-on-Severn on a Pilgrimage to visit the Doddridge tomb where a chaplet was laid in the name of the church. The party visited Abbey Lawn, a house long associated with the Doddridge and Humphreys families and Upton-on-Severn where Philip Doddridge was married to Mercy Maris from the home of her uncle, Ebenezer Hankins. It was a moving and memorable occasion. In 1934 Walter Handel Hall, organist for over forty years, retired from his post as organist and choirmaster. He was publicly thanked for all his devotion to the church through five pastorates; there were, in fact, three members of the choir who who were in it when he first came. He was presented with a silver salver on behalf of the choir and the congregation. In the same year Malcolm Nash, leader of the Young Men's Class and President of No 1 Branch of the National Union of Boot and Shoe Operatives was made a Justice of the Peace. Another retirement that year was that of Frank Godfrey who had served as captain of the Boys' Brigade Company for 25 years; he was succeeded by Dennis G. Webb. In 1939 the Northampton group of Congregational churches was inaugurated at a special service at Castle Hill.

The Girl Guide Company on 7 March 1932. The King's Colour was dedicated by the minister, and is held by Miss Phyllis Preston (Captain).

Pilgrimage to Tewkesbury where lie the remains of Doddridge's widow, Mercy, and five descendants. L to R: Arnold Jeffery, Mrs W. H. Hall, Mrs W. G. Oram, Mrs D. N. Hall, Mrs Doddridge Humphreys, Revd Frank Doddridge Humphreys, Mrs A. E. Rodhouse, Mrs G. Webb,, Miss G. M. Archer, A. B. Calderwood, Revd J. Edmondson and Revd J. E. Tranter.

During the thirties a slum-clearance scheme was put into operation by the Borough Council. Among the buildings demolished in 1934 was the Doddridge Hall, originally known as the Castle Street Mission Hall and presented to the church by H.N.Dixon. On 19 December 1934 many past and contemporary workers attended a final gathering which commemorated fifty years of use for religious and philanthropic work within the neighbourhood. Originally opened by the Revd J. J. Cooper the premises had regularly housed upwards of two hundred scholars. At one time the noted preacher Revd Dr Samuel Hughes had been an energetic worker in this mission the motto of which was, 'The neighbourhood for Christ, and Christ for the neighbourhood'. The Borough Council at the time was toying with the idea of driving a road linking the Mayorhold with the area adjacent to the railway station; it would have passed close to the south facade of Castle Hill Chapel thus making it a prominent landmark.

The A.G.M. on 3 January 1939 heard some salutary comments from the Secretary, D.H.Hall. 'I do not think it is the duty of any secretary to paint a glowing picture when he knows there are some things which are not glowing', he said. Although there had been successes during the year and renovations to the buildings had been successfully completed, a rise in income and three new members promoted from the Junior Membership there was cause for concern. Congregations were low and there was a danger in concentrating effort on the church's organisations to the detriment of other things. The minister agreed and admitted that after all the effort he put into preparing services he often went home disappointed. He wished that the congregations would reach a hundred. The geographical position of the church, he considered, had a great influence on the size of congregations.

The shadow of forthcoming war loomed in an incident in early in 1939 when the Home Office conducted an experimental explosion in Castle Street. Alarmed at damage caused to the church building Messrs Hawtins were called in to examine the structure and consult with the Borough Council. A claim for £10 damage to ceilings and the wall of the schoolroom was agreed by all parties. The eventual outbreak of war in Europe in early September 1939 immediately plunged the church into a crisis situation. Meeting on the 6th the deacons put in hand matters to provide blackout to the buildings, emergency plans in case of air-raids, the use of the basement as a possible shelter, the refilling of first-aid boxes and the removal of the Doddridge relics to a place of safety. Meeting a week later the secretary reported that the military authorities had intimated through the sexton that they would be taking possession of the church buildings within a week. Serious dislocation of the church's activities was envisaged and plans were made to minimise difficulties. A month later discussions were held on the use of the church for providing emergency accommodation for up to a hundred evacuees to the town; this use was felt preferable to military occupation.

Thus began a period of great difficulty. Bernard Godfrey wrote: 'It is no exaggeration to state that [Edmondson's] ministry has been carried on under conditions of greater difficulty than any previous pastorate'. W.G.Oram, the church treasurer, had been warning the church that a financial deficit was building up. Failure to redress the fact that up to two thirds of the congregation did not give regularly for the maintenance of the church's upkeep meant that in 1936 a deficit of over £31 was recorded over a total income/expenditure of £905. By 1940 the deficit had not been cleared and had leapt to £454 in 1943, reaching a peak of £520 the following year. Even in 1948 the deficit was £339. Yet strenuous efforts to raise sufficient cash were made in spite of gross difficulties and the underlying financial position began to slowly improve.

The church meeting on 3 July 1940 noted that 'Mr Arthur E. Wyatt has been called to the colours'. It was to be an all too familiar pattern as the demands of war uprooted men and women from home and church. Not only did the church suffer loss by its young being conscripted, other stalwarts passed away during these dark years. George Webb, shoe manufacturer, died in April 1940 and his funeral was conducted by the minister at Castle Hill. Webb's call to religious and social service began in Henry Cooper's Young Men's Bible Class. He had taught for 32 years in the Mission Hall in Castle Street, was a deacon of the church for 33 years and pioneered the first company of the Boys Brigade in Northampton at Castle Hill. He was a generous supporter of Bethany Homestead. In memory of himself and his wife Amy their children, Dennis, Frank and Dora presented their parents' former home in Kingsley Road to the Y.M.C.A. as its first hostel.

Mr H.N.Dixon

Walter Handel Hall

Walter Handel Hall, a town councillor and head of a firm of yeast merchants died in December 1942. He had been 21 years of age when he was appointed organist at Castle Hill, a position he held for some forty-one years. His funeral at Castle Hill was conducted by the Moderator of the East Midlands Province, the Revd E.M.Drew, assisted by the Revd John Edmondson. A year later, in December 1943, Hugh Neville Dixon's wife Mary died followed in May 1944 by her husband. Mrs Dixon had been an active worker in the church. H.N.Dixon had been a powerful leader at Castle Hill since 1884 when he came to Northampton to assist the Revd Thomas Arnold in his work with deaf-mutes. A distinguished botanist, he was an authority on mosses and his book *A Student's Handbook of British Mosses* was a standard work. A Master of Arts from both Cambridge and London he was a Fellow of the Linnean Society. He had laboured at Castle Hill for 59 years serving as a deacon. He served at county and provincial levels of Congregationalism and was a Director of the London Missionary Society. He was also a leading figure in the foundation of Bethany Homestead and had been chairman of the House Committee. A remarkable man he had skated on the frozen River Nene from Northampton to Peterborough in spite of falling through the ice three times. He had once climbed Snowden three times in a day, and in 1914 had climbed the summit of Mt. Etna sleeping the night on the summit before walking the two miles round the crater the following morning. At the time of his death he was senior deacon at Castle Hill. His beautiful sketches and poetry adding to his scientific expertise and Christian faith meant a deep sense of loss to the church.

Yet despite the difficulties a venture germinated before the war years came to fruition in 1940. For some time a mission outreach had been planned at Bush Hill, on the eastern edge of the town amongst the developing

**Memorial to Hugh Neville Dixon
at Castle Hill**

**Doddridge (Castle Hill)
Congregational Church, c1940.**

housing estates. John Archer relinquished duties at Castle Hill to take on the task of building up a new church. As early as 1935 Archer had urged churches to seek to provide Sunday Schools for the children of families who had removed to the expanding suburbs of the town. As leader of the Northampton Group of Congregational Churches Edmondson had a large share in the inauguration of such missionary work. On 1 March 1944 six members from Castle Hill (Ellen Archer, Gwendoline Underwood, Margaret Jeffery, Nellie Ward, Bertha Claridge and John Archer) were honourably dismissed to help form the new Headlands Congregational Church under the leadership of its new pastor, the Revd Hilda Pettman.

In November 1942 the *Northampton Congregationalist* celebrated its 21st year of publication. Eleven churches in Northampton combined to publish this magazine every month, linking the churches together and expressing common interest and concerns. Its indefatigable editor and major architect of its success was John Archer. H.N.Dixon noted: `...we are in a great degree indebted to Mr Archer, and should like to join in a message of appreciation and gratitude, and to congratulate him on the coming of age of an undertaking that he has nursed from its infancy and seen to grow to full maturity'. Church Secretary for 20 years, secretary and superintendent of the Sunday school, president and secretary of the Ministers and Deacons association plus other duties made Archer one of the greatest leaders within the church. Others like Charles Battle, George Webb, Arthur Jones, William Oram, Alfred Rodhouse, Miss Louisa Robinson, Mrs S.S.Campion and Hugh Neville Dixon provided an outstanding level of dedicated service which held the church together during the dark days of war and its aftermath.

Bernard Godfrey wrote in 1947: `*The congregation has become more widely dispersed than for a century past; the large-scale demolition of slum property around the church and the conditions created by the second world war have greatly effected the working of the church and its organisations. The Sunday School, completely reorganised as a graded school during the early years of Mr Edmondson's ministry, has been reduced to smaller proportions; the Boys' Brigade Company has lapsed; the Men's Own, while remaining an organisation of the Church, now meets at the Central Hall, Abington Square, its numbers during the war, inevitably reduced. Yet, there are gratifying features of this ministry. Before the war, the morning congregations were considerably improved and the evening reasonably maintained. Even during the war congregations suffered less than in many Churches more favourably situated. The activities of what has been known as the Youth Campaign have introduced a number of members of the Church to the work of lay preaching. In the situation in which the Church has found itself, Mr Edmondson has ceaselessly sought to adapt it to the changed and changing conditions of the 20th century'.*

Such changes brought Christians closer together. On 13 September 1945 the Bishop of Coventry (Dr Gorton) together with the secretary of the British Council of Churches (Dr Craig) and the secretary of the Congregational Union of England and Wales (Dr Sidney Berry) took part in a service at Castle Hill. The occasion was the 250th anniversary of the granting of the licence to worship at Castle Hill. It provided an opportunity to look forward to a new era of cooperation and unity. The Bishop of Coventry spoke about the proposed Chapel of Unity to be a part of the new cathedral when rebuilt. He stresses the worldwide nature of the church and was moved by the influence of Castle Hill being one of only two churches still having a licence dating back so closely to the Toleration Act of 1689. In the first of a series of six meetings planned to mark the anniversary Professor Victor Murray declared that it would cost less to rid the world of cancer and tuberculosis than it would to produce the atomic bomb. Other guest speakers included members of the Roman Catholic, Lutheran and Russian Orthodox Churches.

In late February 1947 the two hundred-strong Council of the Congregational Union met in Northampton. During their conference a memorial to Philip Doddridge was unveiled. Traffic was stopped in Sheep Street as members of the Council, civic leaders and local ministers met to unveil the bronze plaque on the building which was Doddridge's Academy from 1740 to 1751. Doddridge had tenaciously fought for freedom in education; Edmondson wrote: `Thus the whole nation owes a debt to this ancient monument and to the spirited little man who inspired its fortunes'.

Members of the Congregational Union, civic leaders and local ministers watch Dr Sydney Berry unveil the plaque on Dr Doddridge's former Academy in Sheep Street. February 1947.

Thumbing through the pages of the minutes of deacons and church meetings there is a distinct impression of the church realising the changes in the society which its sought to serve. In 1946 the church protested to the Minister of Food and the M.P. for Northampton urging that grain be diverted from brewing to use as food. The background was the appalling refugee problem in Europe with millions of displaced people struggling to survive and return to their homes. It was the time when the World Council of Churches was in embryo, and Inter Church Aid was to emerge out of the refugee relief campaign. At national level the Congregational and Presbyterian Churches were talking about union. Times were hard, austerity was the key-word and the church debated whether to restart the *British Restaurant* which had functioned on the premises during the war years. Finance was a problem and valiant efforts were made to 'liquidate the deficiency of income over expenditure'. An annual Gift Day was proposed and ideas such as dimming the lights during the sermon were considered. Guest preachers were encouraged to come but costs proved too expensive. The church was finding it hard to provide the stipend of £400 per annum for the minister and the weekly wage of £4. 5s for Mr Claridge the caretaker. Yet, in spite of the difficulties, the church began to make headway. In August 1947 the numbers of children attending the church rose by some 44 in eight months. The Boys' Brigade Company was restarted (including camp) and a new Guide Leader, Miss M. Latimer, was appointed. The musical tradition of the church, under the impetus of Arthur Hodge, moved forward unabated. Youth activities, generally, improved and the Young Men's Class recommenced. In spite of much pruning the church membership roll showed 145 members. The Handbell Ringing Team, a favourite aspect of the church, was again active and the church did well at the Northampton Choir Festival. An innovation occurred in September 1947 with a baby show, and keeping up with technological innovation the church had its own talkie film shows.

Edmondson worked hard at providing challenging sermon material: *Can Civilisation be Saved?* was a theme for one series of sermons, and *People's Services* and *Come to Church for a Month* campaigns were later commenced in the hope of attracting non churchgoers. For a time the mid-week service was recommenced. Issues such as gambling as well as obtaining sufficient deacons for the church occupied church meeting time. Edmondson involved himself in various evangelistic missions away from Northampton, and was, for example, involved with many other ministers in *The London Commando Campaign* which sought to challenge the Capital with the Gospel. His unremitting labours over twenty years wore away at his health and in 1950

Alfred Rodhouse had to occupy the chair at church meetings due to the pastor's illness. On 30 May the minister's letter of resignation was read out to the church meeting, having been given from the pulpit the previous Sunday. In it Edmondson asked to retire immediately as he could no longer take the strain of the task. The meeting passed the following resolution:

'This Church meeting having heard the letter from the Rev. John W. Edmondson intimating his desire to retire immediately from the pastorate of this Church feels that it has no alternative but to accept the resignation. It desires to express its regret at the continued ill health which has necessitated this step and its earnest hope for improved health in the future. It acknowledges with grateful thanks his ministry during the past twenty years and trusts that he may be given health and strength for further service in the Master's Cause. This resolution was carried unanimously'.

In the parting events the church paid special tribute to their minister's integrity, sincerity and unceasing effort throughout his long ministry, and Mrs Edmondson's quiet ministry in her home on behalf of the church. There is little doubt that no minister in the history of the church at Castle Hill had had to face so many formidable problems as Mr Edmondson.

Revd Frank L. Wallace: 1953 - 1963

Revd Frank Wallace

The *Northampton Congregationalist* for December 1952 remarked: 'Introduced to us by the moderator in these terms - "He is seeking a larger scope" - Rev. Frank L. Wallace, of Mirfield, comes to us on Sunday December 13th. Whether or not he finds that "larger scope" at Doddridge depends on each one of us". At a church meeting held on the 16th the following resolution was unanimously accepted: 'That this meeting of members of the Church of Doddridge (Castle Hill) Church cordially invites the Rev. Frank L. Wallace to be its minister and pledges itself to wholeheartedly support him in his work in the Church and the Town'. Wallace accepted the Call and was inducted on 4 May. The Charge to the Minister was preached by the Rev W. Wallace Lawrence of Crowstone Church, Westcliff-on-Sea and the charge to the Church by former minister of Castle Hill, the Revd R. Morton Stanley (then serving at Wisbech).

Wallace began with a reminder of the nature of the Congregational Church: *'No Person in Authority, no Board or Committee is sending or "settling" a minister on the Church. The members, acting freely together (under God), have felt led to make this move; the minister also comes freely, but under the constraint of Christ. For us the Church is that body of men and women who have bound themselves together in Christian loyalty to work together to deepen our Christian life and fellowship and extend the Kingdom of our Lord. I am sure all of us are reminding ourselves of our great privileges and responsibilities. Tradition, history, buildings, money, can never create a Church. Dedicated people are the Church. Where each brings something of prayer, service, loyalty and love to make the whole complete, we may hope for the Church to flourish and [quoting William Carey] "expect great things from God"'.*

One of the first acts that Wallace performed was in leading the dedication service for the Late Miss Louisa Robinson and the late Mr J. Perry Robinson, two long-standing members of the church who had given devoted service over many years. At the annual meeting in January 1954 encouraging reports showed an improved financial position; although expenditure was £1104 two hundred pounds had been set aside for a Building Maintenance Fund. Thanks to legacies and gifts it had been possible to purchase a manse for the minister, namely 73, Birchfield Road. The Sunday School Annual Meeting was well attended and 'presented reports of a cheering nature'. During the year representations to the Borough Council regarding the redevelopment of the area surrounding the church had been favourably received.

The first anniversary of the new ministry showed a happy church: 'Sunday May 1st, marked the first anniversary of our minister's settlement amongst us. The day was both pleasurable and memorable, with the reception of new members and the recognition of the newly-elected deacons at the Communion service. On the following day Mr Wallace received gifts totalling £130 for Church funds, and members and friends of the church joined in a happy social occasion. The pages of a Doddridge Scrapbook were most ably (and amusingly) turned by Mr Malcolm Nash, and projected on to a screen for all to see by Mr E. Marshall. We enjoyed listening to recordings of the Sunday Half-hour recently broadcast from Doddridge, and the excellent moving pictures of Mr F.E.Webb. Ample refreshmentts were served by the Women's Fellowship, and a happy touch was provided by the Anniversary Cake with its one candle'.

Church life continued throughout the 1950's against the backcloth of improving social conditions nationally; the austerity of the immediate post-war years had begun to give way to better opportunities. Within the vicinity of the church bulldozers and diggers worked away at the reconstruction of the entire neighbourhood; by 1961 the old Boroughs area with its close-packed Victorian terraced streets had been transformed, with the church overlooked by highrise blocks and surrounded by flats and other housing. In March 1957 the *Northampton Congregationalist* noted:

'Meet your neighbours. St Katharine's Court - the new block of flats so much in the public eye during erection - is now open. Our new neighbours are arriving day by day. A "get-together" party has been arranged for the tenants to meet one another, and we hope it may be possible to organise similar occasions in the near future for other residents in the area. We hope to keep the neighbourhood informed about our Church and assure them that Doddridge is a friendly Church where there will always be a welcome'. The venture was a success and new tenants were appreciative of the church's interest in them.

Originally commenced as a money-raising effort the annual May Festivals had a momentum of their own, even though the one for 1955 was held during a blizzard. The availability of more motor cars is reflected in the Mystery Drives held during summer months. Bazaars and other social occasions continued as part of the church's fellowship life. Yet Wallace saw only too clearly the immense challenge that post-war English society had become. The new skyline surrounding the old Meeting House reflected a vast change in outlook:

'It is true that times have changed, that the habits and customs of Edwardian England (often regarded as the heyday of Churchgoing) have gone, never to return. So we have to address the Gospel to a constituency of men and women whose mental and spiritual background is vastly changed. Yet, to this generation we have but one thing to proclaim - the old, old story that "God is Love", and that we can only truly live as we live for Him and by Him'.

In 1957 the Men's Own returned to Castle Hill where the movement had been founded some fifty years previously. In the same year the use of Communion tickets was discontinued. In 1958 due to a decrease in the number of Sunday School scholars during the afternoons the time of Sunday School was changed to 11am. The children met in the church for the opening part of the worship then retired to their classes. 'They will be graded according to age, and it is hoped the Junior Intermediate Group will continue the form of Children's Church Service, so carefully and prayerfully built up over past years. We hope this change will be regarded *as a real attempt to strengthen our hands in staking Christ's claim on the children's lives'.* The new organisation was to be called the Junior Church and has continued in this form until the present.

The most fundamental change made during Wallace's ministry was the gradual uniting of Castle Hill with the Commercial Street Congregational Church. In October 1958 the Northampton Congregationalist recorded under its Doddridge (Castle Hill) column:

'During the past few weeks our deacons have been joining in conversations with the Commercial Street diaconate, whose Church have asked them to consider a possible union with ourselves. These conversations have taken place in a spirit of real understanding and sympathy, and we have indicated that if such a union be decided upon, there will be a willingness to co-operate to the fullest extent, in the hope that any scheme which should emerge should maintain the work and witness of our Commercial Street friends. In the meantime it is hoped to arrange for members of the various organisations to meet each other in their meetings and activities'.

The Commercial Street Congregational Church had been opened on 9 April 1829 at a time when the population of Northampton had doubled since the beginning of the century. The church was built to serve the needs of the town, and was paid for through the generosity of Thomas Wilson of Highbury Independent College, London. Commercial Street Church had been a place of worship drawing a cross-section of Northampton society to its activities. Members of College Street Baptist Church, the Independent Churches at Buckingham and Rothwell together with Mrs M.Abel of Castle Hill were some of the first members of the church. The Revd Charles Hyatt of Castle Hill was amongst the ministers who gathered at the ordination of its first pastor, the Revd Edmund Thornton Prust, on 21 April 1830. Prust was to serve the church for fifty years, exerting a powerful evangelical influence in the town. He initiated the Victoria Road Congregational Church (opened in 1869) paying for the building out of his own pocket.

Union of the Commercial Street and Doddridge Castle Hill) Congregational Churches. June 1959. The procession enters Doddridge Street.

Described as a 'potent influence' Prust initiated joint

Led by the Revds Laurie Wooding and Frank Wallace the procession arrives at Castle Hill.

Communion services between the Northampton Independent churches. Many influential members of Northampton society came to share in the church's activities. Sir Ryland Adkins M.P., for example, was a distinguished member of the church serving it as his father and grandfather had done with great faithfulness. After a run of thirteen Conservative mayors of the Borough a Nonconformist, John Middleton Vernon, was elected Mayor of Northampton in 1868. As a member of Commercial Street the entire Corporation processed to the church for the first civic service ever held in a Northampton Nonconformist church. A succession of able ministers led the church after Prust's retirement in 1881: Revd William Henry Stent (1869-1875), Revd Frederick Wilkins Aveling (1876-1880), Revd Thomas Gasquoine (1881-1892), Revd Anthony Clarke Gill (1893-1896), Revd Henry John Huffadine (1896-1902), Revd Joseph

The Communion Table from Commercial Street serves as a memorial table in the vestibule at Castle Hill

Osborne (1903-1908), Revd Charles Noakes (1909-1915), Revd Harry Lawson (1918-1923), Revd Henry Clifford Vincent (1925-1929), Revd Frank Jennings (1930-1936), Revd William H. Tame (1937-1943), Revd J. Evans James (1944-1952), Revd William H. Tame (1953-1956) and Revd Laurie Wooding (1956-1959).

During the 1930's the church continued to be surrounded by many small dwellings, boasting a good congregation from many parts of the town. A large Sunday school was in operation. However, the immediate area around the church began to suffer change with the demolition of many houses as part of the new town development scheme; the area gradually became more industrialised. After 1945 the general lassitude towards religion meant that congregations

had considerably diminished. The Revd J. Evans James was appointed minister but after his death the church could not afford to call another pastor. Subsequently Mr Tame returned to the town and acted in a part-time capacity until the Revd Laurie Wooding agreed to become honorary part-time minister.

Sadly, the church did not grow numerically although the Sunday School, the Girls' and Boys' Brigades continued as did activities such as the Women's Fellowship and the Sewing Party. It had become increasingly apparent that a decision as to the future of the church would have to be made. The church building was in need of expensive repair work, and the construction of a dual carriageway nearby further isolated the building. Many meetings

The minister's chair from Commercial Street, in the Castle Hill vestibule.

under the leadership of Revd Wooding and the very able secretary, Bert Dawkins, were held. Consultations also took place with Revd Solomons, the Provincial Moderator, initially exploring the possibility of joining with Victoria Road. However, it was unanimously decided that an approach be made to Doddridge (Castle Hill) with a view to uniting the two churches; it was a logical step as the two churches had worshipped together often during the summer months.

At a special church meeting held on 27 May 1959 at Castle Hill and attended by a large gathering the two church secretaries, Bert Dawkins (Commercial Street) and Dennis Hall (Doddridge) outlined the cordial dialogues that had brought the two churches together as co-equal partners in a new enterprise. Propositions were put forward and passed that the two churches be *de facto* one united church with a united ministry, diaconate and with joint officer holders. Bert Dawkins and Frank Webb were appointed joint secretaries, and Dennis G. Webb and Terry J. Barber joint treasurers. Miss May Green became minute secretary, George Tinston room secretary, and Harold Claridge and Will Tebbutt property and equipment stewards. Concluding the business of the meeting the Revd Wallace referred to the Acts of the Apostles when the early church came into being; it was of one mind, one purpose and one accord. 'A church is the fellowship by which Jesus Christ makes himself known', he said, 'This we must remember from this time forward. History is inspiration for the future'.

In a statement to the *Chronicle & Echo* Wallace said:

'Changes in town planning have completely altered the district, the one being intended for industrial development and the other for the erection of council houses and flats. In these circumstances the churches have felt that the wise course is to join their work in one set of premises at Castle Hill. The Commercial Street property will be sold, but it is emphasised that the work of the church and its various organisations will be continued'.

It was agreed that the united church should be known as *Doddridge (Castle Hill) and Commercial Street Congregational Church* but this was later simplified to *Doddridge and Commercial Street Congregational Church*. The deacons of both churches were to remain in office and workers in the Sunday Schools and other youth organisations were to continue in office. The Revd Laurie Wooding was appointed honorary associate minister with the Revd Frank Wallace. On 13 June 1959 a social gathering was held for the last time at Commercial Street. Members and friends joined by representatives of other churches recalled the church's witness over 130 years. Presentations were made by T. J. Barber to Revd Wooding, and by C. F. Palmer to church secretary Bert Dawkins for their outstanding work during a difficult period. On Sunday evening 14 June the final service was held at Commercial Street. Members from Castle Hill joined the Commercial Street congregation at the service led by the Revd Maurice Charles, Principal of Paton College, Nottingham. During the last hymn the ministers walked down the aisles and led the congregation in procession to Castle Hill. Many hearts were heavy at leaving a much loved place of worship but the spirit of new beginnings in a unified church lifted the sadness. Welcomed by the ministers the united congregation filed into Castle Hill for the final prayers and doxology.

On 4 October 1959 the *Celebration of Union* of the two churches was held at Castle Hill. The service was led by the Moderator elect of the Province, the Revd John White. The choir led with the introit, `Blessing, glory, wisdom and thanks' by J.S.Bach. The whole service was underpinned by thanksgiving, and the ancient Church Covenant dating from Thomas Shepard was read by the Revd Wallace:

'We, this Church of Christ, having given up ourselves to the Lord and to one another, do promise and covenant in the presence of God to walk together in all the Laws and Ordinances of Christ according to the Rules of His Gospel, through Jesus Christ so strengthening us'.

Holy Communion concluded the service, an appropriate final act at a vital moment in the church's history.

The united church continued its life of worship and witness, benefitting from the financial resources brought by the Commercial Street Church; in 1958 £640 provided redecoration of the chapel, and in the same year £2097 was placed in the Manse Fund with £4000 being added to the Chapel Fund four years later. As there was a Guide Company at Castle Hill the Girls' Life Brigade from Commercial Street opened a company at Mere Way Infants' School. For a time this was successful but its distance from the church led to difficulties; when the Guide Company closed the Girls Life Brigade transferred to Castle Hill. Wallace reflected the immense changes occurring in the world: *'What can be said about a generation which can place an object on the moon, yet does not know how to place a refugee in a safe world; which can break the barrier of sound, but is confused by the barriers of race and colour; which can explore the heavens, but fears to venture beyond the walls which divide the branches of the Christian church?'*. He was quick to give credit for all the advances of science and technology but *'redemption implies a spirit of reverence and humility before God in the use of His Gifts, shown in an attitude of charitableness towards all his children - even the ones with whom we disagree. This is part of the reason why the Christian faith in its simplicity is so relevant to the exciting times in which we live'*. Wallace urged the church to face up to the great changes in scientific, political and economic patterns of life which the next decade would bring.

1959 saw the passing of two stalwart members of the church; William George Oram and Frank Godfrey had worked together for many years, latterly as life deacons but in earlier years in the Sunday school, the choir, the diaconate and as representatives to the county and other associations. Oram had been a wonderful church treasurer and church secretary; Godfrey had been a faithful Boys' Brigade officer and Sunday School Superintendent. They died within a few weeks of each other. The minister recorded his thanks for the church's provision of a motor car, LNH 899, which was paid for out of the legacy left the church by A. E. Rodhouse. During 1960 worship was conducted upstairs in the schoolroom due to the redecoration of the sanctuary.

On Sunday morning 2 October 1960 the congregation was surprised to see a large cottage loaf and a bunch of grapes on the Communion Table. Having celebrated Harvest Festival the previous week the minister explained that they were a gift from Canon Richards, Vicar of All Saints, from their Harvest Festival. The gift was symbolic of more than friendship between the churches, and as the bread was used during the evening Communion service it underlined the growing gracious relationships between the Anglican and Free Churches of the town. 1961 saw the church taking part in the Week of Prayer for Christian Unity, and welcoming the publication on 14 March of the New Testament section of the *New English Bible*, on the 350th anniversary of the publishing of the *Authorised Version* on 15 March 1611. In 1962 the church shared in the prayers issued by the World Council of Churches meeting at New Delhi under the theme *The Light of the World*. Dr Ernest Payne of the Baptist Union of Great Britain and Ireland, who had presided over the New Delhi Conference, came to preach at Castle Hill in the following May. Outward in its thinking the church involved itself in Inter Church Aid (the forerunner of Christian Aid) in its *Bread for the World Campaign*.

1962 began with a well-attended fellowship meal at which the minister reminded the gathering of the significant dates in the church's history. Treasurer, Dennis G. Webb turned thoughts to the future with the challenge of meeting the church's commitments out of regular giving so that the proceeds of special events could be used for the maintenance and improvement of the premises. This was widely welcomed and, as a result, a *Tercentenary Fund* (1662 - 1962) was opened the first objective of which was the redecoration of the school premises.

Miss May Green, with the Revd Frank Wallace and Revd Malcolm Saunders (St Giles), laying the wreath at the Robert Browne memorial on 24 August 1962. This act commemorated the Great Ejectment of 1662.

The event of outstanding importance in 1962 was the Tercentenary of the Great Ejectment on St Bartholomew's Day 1662 when some two thousand Anglican clergy were forced to leave the Established Church. On that day in 1962 Wallace conducted a service at St Giles where in the churchyard Miss May Green placed a wreath at the Robert Browne Memorial and the Revd Jeremiah Lewis, `one of the 2000', was remembered. The Rev Malcolm Saunders, curate at St Giles led the prayers. In the evening at Castle Hill the Rural Dean of Northampton preached on the need for Unity in Truth as well as love, and the Revd Reginald Baker of College Street Baptist Church spoke on the nation's debt to Nonconformity. A great service was held at College Street on 29 September. It was followed by another at Castle Hill, `the mother church of Northampton Congregationalism' on Sunday 7 October. The services were conducted by the Revd. Dr. H.F. Lovell Cocks (morning) and the Revd. R.T. Brooks (Producer of Religious Broadcasting, B.B.C. Television, London). The Mayor & Mayoress of Northampton, Alderman & Mrs Tompkins together with members of the Borough Council, the Magistrates and representatives of the General Hospital, attended and were greeted by a guard of honour formed by the uniformed organisations of the church. On the following Wednesday the Revd. Dr. Trevor Davies was the guest speaker at a public Tercentenary Meeting which drew Congregationalists from a wide area. Canon Hughes of St Giles, Northampton was the chairman. Writing of the events for the

Northampton Congregationalist Wallace wisely commented on the recent service in St Paul's Cathedral, attended by the Queen, which commemorated the event:

`...the attempt to enforce a uniform pattern of churchmanship in our land served only to create a division between the Established and Free Church pattern of worship...the Archbishop of Canterbury who, recalling this division, went on to pay gracious tribute to the universal debt of the Churches to Nonconformist Theologians and leaders. Amongst some he named as outstanding was Dr Philip Doddridge. In our turn we might remind ourselves of the debt we owe the Prayer Book, whose words we often use, and also rejoice in the witness of devout Anglican Churchmen during the past three centuries...We have every reason to be proud of the heroes of our faith, but this must serve only to make us more desirous in these days to achieve by understanding, what force could not achieve - the Unity of Christian witness that is in accordance with God's Will'.*

Wallace's ministry at Castle Hill was almost over; none expected his announcement in July 1963 that he had accepted a Call to the pastorate of Freemantle Church, Southampton. In the early months of that year he had arranged for the students of Paton College to bring a mission to the neighbourhood. The students were accommodated at Trefoil House by courtesy of the Girl Guides' Association. The mission was called *Free For All* and involved visitation, informal discussions in the coffee bar, films, testimony and preaching. The project was something of an experiment both for the students and the church. It gave a lift to church life after a depressingly hard winter. Although there seemed few results for the visitation of every home in the district seed was sown and the church was encouraged as students and congregation shared in the mission. In the month before Wallace announced his resignation he was discussing the merits of the singing of *Twentieth Century Hymns* which he had included in the Parade Service in June. New popular musical forms and the modernisation of the words of hymns were increasing features of the Christian scene.

At the church meeting on 26 June 1963 Wallace spoke of his move to Southampton. There was a time in both the life of a church and the individual, he said, when a change is necessary. He hoped to start his new ministry in October. Frank Webb said that the church had been fortunate in having Mr Wallace for over nine years. His ministry had been successful and the church was in a much healthier state than in 1953. The church would greatly miss him and his wife who had been a tremendous support. Others spoke of Wallace's influence; Robert Webb remembered the minister's children's addresses which he had enjoyed as a child. As he had grown older he had listened to the minister's sermons with even greater interest. His sermons had contained true words of wisdom. `There are few men who have strong convictions and the ability to put them over'.

Writing in the *Northampton Congregationalist* (October 1963) Mr & Mrs Wallace said their farewell:

`For nearly ten years we have been proud to have been surrounded by the good and gracious people of Northampton - and especially at Castle Hill - who have helped us to engage in a ministry and live our lives. For what you have been, under God, and what we have been able to do together, you have the lasting gratitude of your minister and his wife'.*

Part 8
1965 - 1995
The ministries of Ford, Landon, Diggens and Deacon

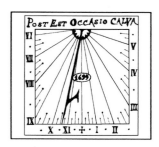

The writing of contemporary history is fraught with problems, not the least being the closeness of the events. The past thirty years of the Castle Hill's history has been a mixture of difficulty and success. Yet out of this period in which British society has undergone even more change, and the world's problems are an ever-present reality, the fellowship meeting on Castle Hill is poised to see the end of the century and the beginning of the third Christian millennium with as much faith and hope as those in the past.

The removal of the Revd Frank Wallace from Northampton in 1963 left the church in a state of pastoral vacancy for several years. A number of possible future ministers came to preach 'with a view' but no settlement was made. Immediately upon being pastorless the deacons arranged for visitation and care of all those within the fellowship. Worship life continued its faithful pattern; on Passion Sunday 1964 the choir sang Eric Thiman's *The Last Supper* with solo parts taken by Angela Allen and Harry Rickard. Such use of the work of an outstanding Congregationalist composer was typical of the continued fine musical tradition of the church. The choir arranged for the St Matthew Singers under their conductor, John Bertalot, to perform in the grounds of Moulton Grange, the home of Mr & Mrs Dennis Webb. In that year the Revd Dennis Heginbotham conducted the Junior Church Anniversary, and Judith Revitt was crowned as May Queen. In October a party visited Mansfield College, Oxford where the Principal, Dr John Marsh, welcomed them and gave a talk on the college and its training of theological students. Ecumenical events proceeded with a Holy Week play in April 1965 being presented by members of All Saints, Castle Hill and College Street churches. St Peter's Church was given leave to use the premises for their Harvest Sale. Cooperation with all the central Northampton churches intensified with efforts to care for local people needing help. New caretakers, Mr & Mrs Warren were appointed to look after Castle Hill and proved themselves very worthy of the task which they continued until 1993. In 1965 an outing was arranged to New College, London where the party was welcomed by the Revd Dr Geoffrey Nuttall and had an opportunity of seeing various relics of Dr Philip Doddridge.

Revd Gordon Ford: 1966 - 1972.

It was, however, the pastorate that most exercised the minds of the deacons, especially in June 1965 when one candidate, the Revd H.E. Johnson wrote declining the invitation. Harold Fussey, secretary, outlined to the church meeting the reasons why Johnson had declined, namely his view that the church needed a team basis for the pastorate, the immediate environment of the church and the nature of the church buildings presenting difficulties for him. He did not see himself fitting in with such a situation. The deacons consulted with the Moderator who outlined examples of how Congregationalism was beginning to work on more corporate lines in other parts of the country. In February 1966 the deacons met with the Revd Gordon Ford of Westcotes Church, Leicester; he subsequently preached at both services on the 20th. He was accepted by the church meeting and by March plans were in hand to acquire a suitable manse and plan the induction service. A manse was purchased, namely 629 Wellingborough Road, for £4500. The induction service was held on 21 May at which the Revd Lovell Cocks was the preacher.

Revd Gordon Ford

Ford's ministry began well, and he threw himself into his work with energy. It was a period in which the church was raising the necessary finance to effect major improvements to the buildings. Towards the end of 1966 plans were well in hand to alter the boiler room and ladies cloakroom, the addition of new toilets, the building up of the floor of the Ladies Parlour, alterations to the passage, vestry, gents' toilet, kitchen and Boys' Brigade Room; altering the existing roof over the old Boys' schoolroom and raising outer walls and stuccoing the brick walls on Castle Hill made the total estimate some £11,500. The whole operation was under the supervision of Frank Webb. These works were gradually carried out. Other ideas were discussed at some length, namely a reversion to the original name of the church as *Castle Hill,* the siting of the Doddridge coat-of-arms on the church building and the naming of the church in large letters on the building. Dennis Webb pressed for a complete modernisation of the entire premises. These schemes did not materialise.

The minister was instrumental in starting the Telephone Samaritans in Northampton; he encouraged a number of church members to take part in its counselling work. He undertook, with the permission of church meeting, a study course in Social Psychology. He took on the chaplaincy at St Crispin's Hospital, and was active with the other town centre churches in furthering ecumenical involvement in projects such as *The people next door* and *The Fish Scheme.* The church presented gifts to Mr & Mrs Ford on the occasion of their Silver Wedding Anniversary in July 1969. Difficulties arose within the fellowship and centred upon the minister who offered the deacons his resignation. The church meeting voted by a majority to ask him to stay; although several people resigned from their posts the life of the church continued. In the background the denomination as a whole was moving towards the creation of union with the Presbyterian Church. Nearer to home the scrapping of the proposed highway that would have passed across the front of the church linking the Mayorhold and Chalk Lane was welcomed. By the end of the year, with the deletion of 29 members from the membership roll, deaths and transfers the number of members stood at 115. Finance, however, remained a worry and strenuous efforts were being made to maintain healthy financial balances.

On 5 September 1971 a special church meeting heard the minister read a statement of his resignation. He had hoped, he said, to have had a ministry of some ten years at Castle Hill. Two years previously he had offered his resignation and the church had by a large majority wanted him to stay. It had become clear that the minority would not accept the will of the Church and this had resulted in resignations, defections and a policy of non-cooperation. He had accepted the Call to the new united pastorate of Clermont & Lewes Road Congregational Churches, Brighton. Mr & Mrs Ford left for Brighton after a farewell gathering at Castle Hill. He was inducted to his new pastorate on 5 February. In the wake of this unhappy episode in the church's history a number of leading members of the church defected. Yet this led the way to a new beginning and gave opportunity for a fresh approach. Surveying the diminished congregation Dennis Webb, with typical optimism, declared that the church would go on regardless of the difficulties. Under the temporary interim moderatorship of the Rev Robert Murray the church elected new officers with Arthur Wyatt as chairman of church meetings, Dennis Webb as church secretary, Fred Bird as treasurer and Roy Embrey as property steward. The Revd Ford died on 23 August 1990 in his early seventies.

The United Reformed Church

In 1972 two church structures were buried in order that a new and living church could offer its life and witness as part of the Church Catholic and Reformed both in the United Kingdom and the world. The Congregational Church in England and Wales and the Presbyterian Church of England were thus co-joined. No sooner had this marriage been enacted than a third party - the Churches of Christ - showed great interest in opening negotiations with the new United Reformed Church. This was to lead to their uniting in 1981. That three bodies so disparate in history and tradition should become one united church is a remarkable occurrence of far greater complexity than the uniting of Methodism in 1932 or even the Scottish Union of 1929.

Attempts had been made, even before the Restoration in 1660, by Presbyterians and Congregationalists to co-operate in the *Common Fund*. In 1672 a weekly lecture was established at the Pinner's Hall in London. Encouraged by the Toleration Act of 1689 the *Happy Union* was founded `in and about London' two years later. Yet by the end of the century doctrinal disputes had soured relationships, the Presbyterians founding a rival meeting at the Salter's Hall in 1694; the Congregationalists left the Common Fund the following year. Disputes over subscription to Trinitarian credal statements led to further division in the early 18th century; only figures like Doddridge could make a stand for toleration seeking (as Alexander Gordon vividly expressed) to `obliterate old party lines' and `unite Nonconformists on a common religious ground'.

At the heart of the differences between Presbyterianism and Congregationalism lay a differing understanding and approach to the doctrine of the Church. `For the Congregationalist the Church was first local having a universal dimension to which the oneness of Christian experience bore undeniable witness...For the Presbyterian the church was primarily universal whose local outcrops were bound to acknowledge not only each other but their common source in the One Rock'.(A. MacArthur: *The Background to 1972*). Although these differences were rarely articulated nor rigidly defined they lay behind the different use of language such as `congregation' or `church', or formed attitudes regarding who makes a minister and whose minister he is, and the source of authority and decision making in the church. Trust Deeds, Creeds and Confessions encapsulate these differing perceptions.

The new Presbyterian Church of England (re-formed in 1876) took immense sustenance from the revival within Scottish Presbyterianism and the immigration of many Scots south of the border. Many saw the next step as amalgamation with the Congregationalists. Yet it was not until 1932 that conversations began; they continued until the outbreak of war disrupted the discussions until 1945. Six years later an *Act of Covenant* was made, and from 1963 a joint advisory committee slogged away at facing the difficult issues: with uneven spread across England and Wales, with Presbyterianism absent from many villages and the South West yet strong in many towns and cities, with a decline of fifty village chapels per annum, problems seemed formidable. During the 1960's Congregationalism underwent a process of self-examination which resulted in a significant decision to take a more `catholic' and less rigidly independent stance; the Congregational Union (dating from 1831) became the Congregational Church in 1966, each local church being a free covenanting member.

In 1967 a joint *Declaration of Faith* and a brief confession were formulated; they were widely accepted. It now depended on the voting of the two assemblies meeting in London and Newcastle-upon-Tyne, and the voting by each local Congregational church across the land. At Castle Hill on 1 December 1971 the church meeting assembled to vote on the resolutions:

1. `That this Church resolves to unite with other member churches of the Congregational Church and with congregations of the Presbyterian Church to form one United Church under the name of the United Reformed Church (Congregational-Presbyterian) in England and Wales by the procedures and upon the basis, terms and conditions and provisions and with the Ministry Structure and Councils defined and declared in the Scheme of Union.

2. That the result of the voting be conveyed by the minister or church secretary to the Revd John Huxtable forthwith'.

Thirty-seven voting papers were issued, and thirty-seven were returned with 31 for the propositions and six against. The percentage majority of 83.78 met the critical majority of 75% required. It was a fitting conclusion to Ford's ministry at Castle Hill, the meeting being his last. The overwhelming voting of the two separate assemblies meeting in London and Newcastle-upon-Tyne in favour of union, and the wait for the results from every local Congregational church followed by the ratification by the two assemblies in 1972 led to great excitement. The climactic Uniting Service on 5 October of that year, televised from Westminster Abbey during the day and celebrated at the City Temple in the evening, are all part of the Church's history. It marked the first union of two distinct Christian denominations in the United Kingdom since the Reformation. On 26 September 1981 the Reformed Association of the Churches of Christ was also bought into the United Reformed Church adding another unique strand to the new church.

In a sermon preached on 8 October 1972 at Castle Hill (the first occasion of church worship following the formation of the United Reformed Church and also the church's anniversary) the Revd Dr Geoffrey Nuttall of New College, London commented:

'...the U.R.C. brings together in a single community two streams of Free Church tradition and conviction: and broadly speaking, what the Presbyterians have represented was order, orderliness, and the assurance of a true and trustworthy framework, while we Congregationalists have represented freedom, spontaneity and the hopefulness of an expectant flexibility. There have been other differences, of course; but the main distinction of emphasis and ethos lies somewhere there. Now the things represented on both sides, all of them are good; the difficulty has been to see how, humanly speaking, all could be represented at once, and the right mixture or balance found. This is what it is hoped, and believed, has now been found in the new union; but it will be so, as, and only insofar as our text 'for the love of Christ constraineth us' is held fast, and held high as the motto of the new Church: so that we accept, and expect, the element of constraint and restraint, of order and of law, within and in accordance with the love of Christ, which also supplies the element of forward-looking waiting upon the Spirit of God which cannot be bound or subject to the laws of man'.

In the meantime Revd Laurie Wooding had agreed to be interim moderator at Castle Hill, taking over from Arthur Wyatt who had held the fort since the departure of Rev Murray in August. At the annual meeting a review was held of what had been a traumatic year. The Church Roll stood at 100 members. Faithful people like Harold Claridge had passed away and in his and his sister May's memory a memorial fund was established in order to restore the old vestry. In spite of the transfer of seven members away from the church others had ably stepped in to fulfil the necessary tasks; Angela Allen took over as choir leader and Esme Stone became the new organist. No less than 48 preachers had served the church during the vacancy, and relations with other local churches remained very cordial; indeed, discussions had been initiated by College Street as to a possible closer cooperation between the two churches. The church had been officially represented at the final Assembly of the Congregational Church and at the Service of Thanksgiving at Westminster Abbey. As the secretary reported:

Following the enactments in London we as a Church came to worship on October 8th and under the guidance of Rev. Geoffrey Nuttall, we engaged ourselves to be part of this new Church. A memorable service, based upon the eminent preacher's theme: For the love of Christ constraineth us brought us into a realisation of our newly born Church and we found ourselves committed to a broader path of Church Government, a way which we now continue to explore'.

By the close of 1972 a new election of elders, replacing the former category of deacons, took place. It was only possible to elect eight of the twelve places required. On 14 January 1973 the first Moderator of the General

Assembly of the United Reformed Church, Revd John Huxtable, came as guest preacher to Castle Hill. It was an historic occasion as he ordained the Castle Hill elders at the communion service, the very first elders to be so commissioned in the United Reformed Church.

Revd J. Richard Landon 1973 - 1976

Revd Richard Landon

By the close of 1972 the name of the Revd Richard Landon had been brought to the notice of the church. Coming from a strong Congregational family resident in Newcastle-under-Lyme he had been at university for three years and was in his final year at Mansfield College, Oxford. He came to visit Castle Hill on 7 January 1973. On 20 June the church meeting unanimously accepted the elders' recommendation `that we invite Mr Richard Landon to meet [us] with serious intent for the pastorate'. Landon and his wife Elizabeth visited the church. On 3 September the District Council of the URC gave him its formal approval of the Call. On 6 October he was duly ordained and inducted to the pastorate. The Moderator, Revd John White was assisted by Revd Laurie Wooding the Chairman and Secretary of the District Council and the Chairman of the Northampton Council of Churches. The Revd. Dr.Norman Goodall was preacher. A suitable manse was purchased by the church, namely 80 Winchester Road, Delapre.

Landon was concerned to make himself and the church better known in the neighbourhood, to help members get together informally for Bible study and for the deepening of Christian faith, and to bring young people into the fellowship of the church. New youth work was commenced with John Singlehurst as leader. Membership had dropped to 86 and concern was being expressed at building up the numerical strength of the fellowship. Nevertheless, there was in the church a loyalty and commitment to discipleship upon which the future would be built. The quiet, steady input of work by many in the church was its strength. In November 1974 a visitation of the neighbourhood was held; it was a preliminary to a more ambitious effort in the following year entitled *Come Alive in `75'*. More than a dozen students led an exciting and memorable mission in the vicinity of the church. The students were accommodated by church members; visits to the youth organisations of the church and to local schools plus a coffee bar and special services filled a very busy ten day schedule in September 1975. Landon took on the editorship of *Castle Hill News*, provided a new duplicated format and encouraged the young people to lend a hand in its production.

Landon's ministry at Castle Hill proved to be short in extent, although his youthful enthusiasm greatly encouraged many. He and his wife, Liz, left in February 1977 after a three year ministry. He had accepted a Call to the church at Shrub End, Colchester. At the farewell gathering tributes were given by Will Tebbutt, Esme Stone, the Revd Ken Thomason and the Revd David Wilson. On behalf of the church members Agnes Tarry presented a floral arrangement to Mrs Landon, and Arthur Wyatt presented an inscribed silver tray and cheque to Richard Landon. The good wishes expressed to them as they prepared for their new sphere of service in Colchester were intermingled with reminiscences of the three past years, especially the contribution to the musical side of church life.

1977 - 1983

Dennis G. Webb

The church settled into a period which was to be the longest pastoral vacancy in its entire history. For six years the church was without a minister, but during that time a faithful band of members kept the essential life of the church continuing and developing. The Revd Dennis Heginbotham accepted the role as Interim Moderator and, from the outset, urged the church to stay loyal to what God willed for His church rather than seek to pursue personal ways. It was a message that was heeded. 'Where were you?' he bluntly asked when only ten members turned up for a church meeting. If a 71 year old could make it from some distance where were the rest of the able-bodied members? Attendance at church meetings had been poor for some time and Heginbotham challenged every member to play their part at 'a time of great importance for the fellowship'. Wider discussions within the District Council were questioning the viability of a full-time ministerial post for the church, given its relative decline. In March 1978 the news that it was proving impossible to group Doddridge & Commercial Street URC with another church came as a welcome breath, but the

likelihood that a future full-time minister would probably have to be shared with another church was not so acceptable.

The quiet influence of Dennis Webb was one of the factors which held the church together during the long interregnum. Another product of the influential Young Men's Bible Class, led by Henry Cooper, he had already given a lifetime of service both to the Church and to the Boys' Brigade. He wisely saw that the church needed another celebration upon which to focus, an event that would remind it of its history and impel it towards a hopeful future. The ideal moment presented itself in the 250th anniversary of the ordination of Philip Doddridge to Castle Hill on 19 March 1730. With incredible energy, at the age of 77, he set about planning a suitable celebration. A

Malcolm Deacon with the Chairman of the County Council (Cllr John Poole O.B.E.) and Mrs Poole at the launch of *Philip Doddridge of Northampton*, March 1980.

committee was formed in 1978 with less than two years to do its work. His skill in pulling together the talents and enthusiasm of many people brought in John Poole, John Thornton and Malcolm Deacon. Out of the discussions emerged a workable and ambitious plan.

A series of lectures was given by Geoffrey Nuttall, Ernest Payne, Alan Everitt, Stephen Mayor and Victor Hatley and later published by the University of Leicester (*Philip Doddridge, Nonconformity and Northampton* 1981). Northamptonshire Libraries published *Philip Doddridge of Northampton* by Malcolm Deacon (1980), which reached a wide circle including the Queen Mother and Dr Billy Graham and received much acclaim. The British Tourist Board and the Northampton Development Corporation produced a tourist guide map of the town featuring the Doddridge Trail. Stickers, broadsheets and other publicity material were also produced. The Education Department produced a special Doddridge pack for all schools. The church also ordered a hundred dozen commemorative mugs which kept selling until 1994. The Borough Council provided special exterior lighting to the church for several months and took the opportunity of clearing up much of the derelict land that surrounded the church, turning it into much needed car parking spaces.

Webb's idea of a special play on the life of Philip Doddridge did not materialise but special commemorative music entitled *In the Beginning* (based upon St John's Gospel 1: 1 - 5) was written by Will Yeomans and performed in the Northampton General Hospital chapel by the Chamber Orchestra of the Northamptonshire Music Schools and conducted by John Frith. A number of radio and television programmes ensued from the Doddridge biography, and a major exhibition on Doddridge was mounted by the Museum in Guildhall Road. The local press carried a stream of reports. Special services were held throughout 1980 at Castle Hill, and also at the Chapel at the General Hospital, founded by Doddridge in 1744. The Celebrations' Committee erected a brass plaque on the wall of the original infirmary in George Row; this was dedicated by Malcolm Deacon. Of special memorial must be the service on the morning of 23 March when the 900 seating capacity of the church was fully used. Some fifty representatives of the County Council in full ceremonial robes accompanied the Mayor and Mayoress and the Chairman of the County Council. Five hundred Boys' and Girls' Brigade members with their bands paraded to the church. At the evening service eighteen URC and Congregational churches from the town, county and beyond were represented. The services were led by the Revd Robert Latham and assisted by Revd Denis Heginbotham. The Hinckley Church where Doddridge preached his first sermon was represented and friends from Nuneaton also attended. At an ecumenical service on 13 April six other denominations were present to hear the Revd Bernard Thorogood (General Secretary of the URC) preach. During May a Flower Festival concluded these notable events.

Revd Wilfred Diggens 1982 - 1991

Revd Wilfred Diggens

Castle Hill News for the period 1981 -1983 breathes the air of a church beginning to revitalise. The recent celebratory events had certainly regenerated enthusiasm and had begun a process of renewal. The Interim Moderator, Revd Denis Heginbotham, kept a steady influence for good until he retired from the post in the summer of 1981; a visit by members of Castle Hill to his former church at Newport Pagnell, recently restored after a disastrous fire, inspired not a few. Heginbotham was succeeded by the Revd Barry Jones of Duston, and the church was visited by the Provincial Moderator, the Revd John Slow. The Revd David Watson of York, one of the foremost evangelists of recent times, led an ecumenical Christian Festival in the town during 1981; he visited Castle Hill where he showed great interest in the Doddridge memorabilia. In 1982 the URC Churches Luncheon commenced.

On Advent Sunday 1982 the Revd Wilfred Diggens commenced his ministry at Castle Hill. On the previous day he had been ordained during a splendid service at which the Moderator of the Thames North Province of the URC, the Revd Michael Davies, emphasised that it was a new beginning for the church and a time of spiritual challenge for the whole fellowship. Wilfred Diggens was born in 1920 so came to the ministry at an age when most people retire. Yet he brought an enthusiasm and energy few could emulate. His wife Gladys fully supported him in his work and the two frequently visited together. `We are hoping that our services will continue to show some increase in numbers - even if some only come out of curiosity to see what sort of man you have found after six years waiting and looking', he commented in the 1983 New Year edition of *Castle Hill News*. Diggens had been a commercial traveller within the hardwear industry all his life, but had been a lay preacher and youth leader in London for many years. In 1965 he had decided after a meeting at the Islington Sunday School Union to become a lay preacher; he then became a lay pastor giving service to churches in Burnham and at Harecourt, Islington. He brought a lifetime of experience and always regarded himself as `a salesman for Jesus Christ'.

Diggens was concerned that the church should reach out into the community and changed *Castle Hill News* into a newsletter format. *`We have a good magazine, thanks to the promptings and efforts of the editor'*, he wrote, *`but does it reach to all parts of the fringe of the fellowship. Does it go into the homes of all our young people? Does it go into the homes of those who have links with Doddridge but are not yet aware that we have begun a new chapter in our history? Take one to them'*. He was concerned to meet people and initiated the Wednesday Meeting Point coffee morning as a means of keeping in touch with the local community. Many will recall the urn boiling away and steaming up the Boys' Brigade Room which was used for these occasions. Another innovation was the Bring a Guest services which were aimed at interesting outsiders in the church. During 1982 Lyndon Vizard had requested that a youthful group within the church should be allowed to lead worship with their musical instruments; he had promised the elders that the group wouldn't be `too noisy'. The group became known as *Discovery* and have continued until the present time to be an important part of the church's worship.

For his eight year ministry at Castle Hill Diggens kept up an unremitting effort to build the church both numerically and spiritually. He encouraged a Prayer Pyramid. In January 1988 the eldership was increased from ten to twelve in an attempt to provide more visitation of the congregation. He believed in `Friendship Evangelism' and his 76 newsletters published during his ministry expressed a newsy style that valued each individual. He was particularly keen to build up the young people's and children's work of the church, and strengthened links with the local primary school, Spring Lane Lower School. He was also supportive of links with Parkside Independent School and welcomed their contribution to the life of the church. Ecumenically he was a keen supporter of cooperation between the Town Centre Churches, and encouraged joint Bible studies and enthusiastically took part in the Ecumenical Assembly held in 1990 at the Spinney Hill Hall. In 1990 the British Council of Churches changed to The Churches Together in England, another historic moment in ecumenical development; the active participation by the Roman Catholic Church was welcomed, not just nationally but at Castle Hill too. In February 1990 the area around the church was renamed the Spring Boroughs and a drop-in centre was opened in Beaumont Court. Two years earlier the church had distributed a thousand leaflets in the area, and contact with local residents was always a prime concern.

During his ministry the church's financial position began to move `from deficit into balance and into a healthy surplus', although he stressed that no-one should ever be complacent. An appeal for £30,000 was launched in order to finance repairs and redecoration of the premises and the church membership rose to the occasion which saw the redecoration of the sanctuary and other parts of the premises, including repairs to roofs and guttering. During this work worship was held in the schoolrooms. He wrote in March 1989: *`On the first Sunday we had a wonderful sense of togetherness, and we hope that everybody will continue to support the services until we return to the Sanctuary. Its reopening will be a witness to the Town that our fellowship, the oldest Free Church in Northampton, is alive and well, and things are happening. Let us praise God together'*. Always keen to increase congregations he urged members to use their cars as `gospel chariots' to bring in those who had transport difficulties; Sunday bus services into town concerned him, a long-standing problem for all town centre churches. Within the fellowship he urged greater attendance at church meetings and regular worship. Gradually the membership of the church rose until it reached ninety at the close of his ministry in March 1991.

Diggens was conscious of the heritage of the church and its place in the history of Nonconformity. The church welcomed the Historic Churches Annual Sponsored Bike-ride and Walkabout. In May 1989 the Borough Council fixed a metal plaque to the East wall of the church in Doddridge Street commemorating the work of Philip Doddridge and the church's history. 'We are stewards of an ancient Free Church heritage', he declared, 'but the real heritage stems from Easter, Pentecost, Christ and the Holy Spirit. It is still moving among us today'. In November 1990 the East Midlands Provincial Synod met at Castle Hill and the minister was proud to host the occasion. 'Our redecorated premises, the standard of the catering, the speedy service and the smooth running of it all set a new high standard for Synod'. It was a fitting climax to one who had sought to bring together the local URC churches in the United Reformed Churches Committee, had served as Interim Moderator at Harrold URC, and was keenly interested in the developing venture of a National URC Youth Centre at Yardley Hastings.

In July 1990 he wrote that his second extension of his ministry beyond the age of 65 would end in the following June: *'Age is just a figure on a birth certificate or a state of mind. I am glad that in my sixties I was not prematurely old, perpetually sleepy or obsessed with impending old age. Some say that life begins at forty - for me life is beginning at 70! With every day a new opportunity, wondering in what new ways the Lord will lead me'.* He announced that he would retire from the pastorate and led his last service on 3 March 1991. Typical of the man he was inducted to a one third part-time ministry at the Cowper Memorial Church in Olney where his unbounded energy led to a transformation of their premises and a growth in membership. Tragically, a long illness throughout 1994 led to his death on Boxing Day. His funeral on 9 January 1995, led by the Revd Malcolm Hanson the Provincial Moderator, was attended by a large congregation anxious to pay their last respects to 'Wilf'.

Revd Malcolm Deacon 1991 -

Revd Malcolm Deacon

On 24 March 1991 the Revd Malcolm Deacon led the Palm Sunday morning service at Castle Hill. He was a student at Westminster College Cambridge, completing a year of extra training in order to transfer from the non-stipendiary to the stipendiary ministry. Deacon had had a successful career in education, having been headmaster of schools in Duston and Kingsthorpe. Coming from a Baptist background in Kettering he had moved to Duston in 1972 at the time of the formation of the United Reformed Church. He had been a lay preacher from the age of sixteen and had served the Duston Church for some nineteen years as well as the wider District as a lay preacher. Over the years he had preached at Castle Hill many times. He had been ordained at the Duston Church on 4 May 1988 and had since served that church as Assistant Minister. In 1990 he had decided to 'retire' from teaching and had spent the following year at Cambridge. Ready to serve the United Reformed Church he and his wife Stephanie waited for a Call. It came from Castle Hill in the form of a document signed by 83 members of the church and congregation. The work done years before on the Castle Hill archives, leading to the Doddridge Celebrations of 1980 had turned full circle and now he had returned as the church's minister. He was inducted to the pastoral office on 31 August 1991, the presiding minister being the Revd Alasdair Walker, Acting Moderator of the East Midlands Province of the URC. For the first three years of his ministry his pastorate was shared with the Methodist Church at Wootton. This became a local ecumenical project in 1994 being a joint venture between the Methodist Church and the United Reformed Church and known as the Wootton Trinity Christian Centre. From 1 January 1995 Deacon became full-time pastor of Castle Hill in recognition of the growth of the church. He combines chaplaincies to Nene College and Parkside School alongside being deputy co-ordinator for the Clergy Response to Major Disasters within the County of Northamptonshire, and other duties within the wider U.R.C.

Exterior view of Doddridge & Commercial Street United Reformed Church. 1994.

Discovery. 1991

Numerical growth of the church has continued together with the development of new expressions of fellowship life. Morning Prayers every Wednesday have become a regular feature of the worship life of the church. Bible Studies are well-attended. Attendances at worship steadily improve and there is a general change in a social milieu that brings hope for the future. More people from the neighbourhood are attending the church. A new awareness is growing of the need for the church to be a family in a social scene that is devoid of so much care. Well established organisations such as the Bright Hour and the Brigades, the Junior Church and the Choir continue their dedicated contribution, as do many individuals. New church members are finding their way into the church's life and are beginning to effect change within a stable framework. The discussion of Vision 2000 and the way the church is being led by God is all part of a challenging period in the church's ongoing life. Yet it has to be left to a future historian to assess the closing years of the 20th century and the commencement of another. In the 300th year of the church's worship on Castle Hill it has been thought right to revert to its original name; thus from the 1 January 1995 the church became known as Castle Hill United Reformed Church. As the church begins its fourth century of witness emphasis is being made on the place where we worship, the continuity of Christian fellowship and the faithfulness of the whole people of God over many generations. We wait on God and take heart from the motto which the original builders carved on the ancient sundial: `post est occasio calva'. Opportunity must still be grasped if we are to go forward.

Interior view of Doddridge & Commercial Street United Reformed Church. 1994. From 1 January 1995 the church reverted to its original name of Castle Hill (United Reformed Church) honouring still the memory of Philip Doddridge but also the thousands of others who have been and still constitute the fellowship of this place of worship.

A changing name but a faithful continuity over three centuries:

1695 Castle Hill Meeting.
1862 Doddridge Chapel (Congregational).
1959 Doddridge & Commercial Street Congregational Church.
1972 Doddridge & Commercial Street United Reformed Church.
1995 Castle Hill United Reformed Church

Select Bibliography.

Manuscript Sources:

The sources consulted for this volume are held by the Castle Hill United Reformed Church, Northampton. They comprise the Church Book (1694) and subsequent records, registers, minute books, letters, unpublished manuscripts, financial statements, photographs and other artefacts connected with the church's history.

Printed Sources:

Archer J. *The Story of a Century* (Archer and Goodman 1910) The story of the Castle Hill Sunday School from 1810 to 1910.

Arnold T. and Cooper J. J. *The History of the Church of Doddridge* (Kettering and Wellingborough, Northamptonshire Printing and Publishing Company., 1895). A detailed account of the church's history up to 1895.

Campion S. S. *A Chapter in Local Religious History* (Archer and Goodman 1929) A brief but detailed history of Commercial Street Congregational Church up to 1929.

Deacon M. *Philip Doddridge of Northampton* (Northamptonshire Libraries 1980). The life of Philip Doddridge within the context of his times and particularly Northampton. Detailed bibliography of all Doddridge's writings and other sources relating to Nonconformist history.

Gasquoine T. and others. *The History of Northampton Castle Hill (now Doddridge) & its Pastorate with reports on the Bi-centenary Services.* (Northampton 1896)

Nuttall G. F.(ed) *Calendar of the Correspondence of Philip Doddridge, D.D. 1702 -1751* (Northamptonshire Record Society and the Royal Commission on Historical Manuscripts, 1979)

Printed manuals, magazines, newsletters, orders of service and other material are kept within the church's archives.

Roll of Ministers, Castle Hill:

1672 - 1695	Samuel Blower		1884 - 1904	Joseph Cooper
1695 - 1696	Thomas Shepard		1901 - 1903	Charles Davie (assistant minister)
1699 - 1709	John Hunt		1905 - 1910	William Pierce
1709 - 1729	Thomas Tingey		1911 - 1917	R. Morton Stanley
1729 - 1751	Philip Doddridge		1918 - 1930	John E. Evans
1734 - 1741	Job Orton (assistant minister)		1931 - 1951	John Edmondson
1753 - 1760	Robert Gilbert		1954 - 1963	Frank Wallace
1762 - 1775	William Hextal		1965 - 1969	Laurie Wooding (hon. associate minister)
1777 - 1827	John Horsey		1966 - 1971	Gordon Ford
1827 - 1833	Charles Hyatt		1973 - 1976	Richard Landon
1833 - 1859	John Bennett		1982 - 1991	Wilfred Diggens
1860 - 1882	Thomas Arnold		1991 -	Malcolm Deacon
1879 - 1882	John Oates (assistant minister)			

Appendix 1: The Sundial

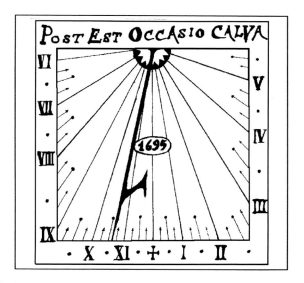

The sundial at the Castle Hill Church carries a date of 1695; it is quite possible that this dial has been there since that time, but in regard to the rebuilding of the Meeting House in c1718 it may well have been rebuilt into the new wall. The sundial has all the features of a contemporary 17th century design, although the dial face has now mostly worn away. The gnomon is intact and is most likely original. The dial is unusual in that it has been designed to work on a wall that declines (or faces) a few degrees East of South. This has a number of implications. Firstly, although the dial would show a full 12 hours, it would be from approximately 5.45am to 5.45pm. It was traditional not to show on the sundial those hours that the sun could never reach, which is why VI is absent in the afternoon. Secondly, the hour lines on a declining sundial are not symmetrical about the vertical Noon line as they would be on a direct South facing dial. It required a knowledge of Trigonometry to calculate their position. Thirdly, the gnomon would no longer be mounted vertically. The gnomon springs from the top of the Noon line but the foot of the support needs to be a small distance to the left of this line. This again needs to be calculated.

The vast majority of church sundials mounted on walls which don't face exactly South are direct dials `tilted' at an appropriate angle to face South. These are much easier to calculate, and examples can be found on the village churches at Chipping Warden and Chacombe. The designer of the Castle Hill sundial took no such short cuts. The dial displays skilled design and craftsmanship. A close inspection reveals that, even after 300 years, there are still some traces of the incised hour lines. These show that the dial originally had hour, half-hour and quarter-hour lines. For the purposes of producing the illustration and its hour lines, these have been calculated for the location Latitude 52 degrees 14 minutes North, and Longtitude 00 degrees 54 minutes West; map reference SP750605, sheet 152, OS *Landranger* series.

The inscription, a Latin motto, is rather more optimistic than the frequently melancholic mottoes our predecessors were fond of. It is a shortened version of a Latin hexameter written by the Roman poet Cato: `Fronte capillata post est occasio calva'. This has been translated rather literally by Gatty & Lloyd in their book *Sundials* (1896) as: `Opportunity has locks (i.e. hair) in front, but is bald behind'. Another translation might be: `Take time by the forelock'.

It is not known who designed or constructed the sundial although it is possible that Noble & Butlin who were local map and sundial makers, and who were associated with the Castle Hill might well be the originators. They certainly possessed the skills necessary. Although the hour lines were cut into the stone and could have worked alone, it is quite likely these were intended to be a permanent guide for those who painted the dial. Traditional colours for sundials of this era were blue, gold and black. Newly painted, this sundial would have been a magnificent sight on a sunny day.

Based mainly upon information supplied by Colin Lindsay, British Sundial Society. 26 January 1995.

Appendix 2. Nonconformist Burials.

When the Meeting House was erected in 1695 it was built on part of the land once occupied by St Mary's Church and burial ground; the only visible remains left is the stone wall along part of Chalk Lane. For a century or more after the closure of St Mary's in 1539 `Le Castelle Grene' lay undisturbed. The burial ground for the Meeting House seems to have been a continuation of the St Mary's cemetery. The first recorded burial took place in 1707. Early burial registers are incomplete; it was not necessary in law to record burials. Some 530 burials are accounted for, and it is estimated that the number of burials on the site must be in excess of a thousand. Child burials were done without ceremony, and many were deaths were due to epidemics of smallpox, diptheria and cholera. In order to use up the surplus of wool most burials during the 1760's used woollen shrouds; the use of lace or cotton required extra payment.

During the history of Castle Hill the burial ground was altered in shape and size, so it is impossible to find individual graves. No burials are recorded for the years 1790 - 1797. The gravestones and memorials that have survived date from the 19th century and few are in their original places. The memorial slab to William Ager, for example, set in the garden wall adjacent to Chalk Lane was originally situated near the gates in Quart Pot Lane. Until 1852 there was no public provision for the burial of Nonconformists. They had rights of burial in Parish churchyards in unconsecrated ground, but funeral services were withheld particularly for the unbaptised. The growth of population led to the filling up of churchyards so that in the 1840's the Inspector of Nuisances decreed that new burial grounds be opened where necessary. Burial Boards were compelled to divide cemeteries into consecrated and unconsecrated areas marked by wide paths, or provide separate burial grounds. Dissenting ministers conducting funerals were refused any fees.

By the 1830's the burial ground at Castle Hill was virtually full so a new place for Nonconformists was urgently needed. At this time private cemetery companies were being formed, so land was purchased by leading Nonconformists in Billing Road and the Northampton General Cemetery Company was formed in

April 1846. 1000 shares at £10 each were issued, and leading Northampton Nonconformists and especially from Castle Hill were prominent in the venture. As Nonconformists clearly advocated equal rights to women it is interesting to note that within a year the new company had women shareholders. The General Cemetery Company went into liquidation in 1959 and was taken over by the Northampton Corporation in 1962. Many of the prominent members of Castle Hill are buried there: the Jeffery family, John Robinson, Mr Pressland of Pressland Stores in the Drapery (later Adnitts, then Debenhams) and William Pitt, the first captain of the 1st Northampton Boys' Brigade Company. A huge obelisk at the cemetery commemorates the life of the Revd Thomas Arnold. Naturally, as the church building was expanded, especially in 1862 much of the burial ground surrounding the church was used up. Work on the Memorial Garden in 1992-3 revealed human remains and a brick-built tomb.

Doddridge's travelling pulpit. Discovered at Creaton United Reformed Church and presented to Castle Hill in 1994.

Appendix 3:
The Doddridge Travelling Pulpit.

During 1993-4 the Creaton United Reformed Church celebrated its Tercentenary. As part of its concluding acts of worship the minister of Castle Hill, Revd Malcolm Deacon, led worship and was presented with a travelling pulpit which was used by the Revd Philip Doddridge on occasions when he preached on the village green. The pulpit was duly transported to Castle Hill where it stands in the north-east corner of the church. Deacon had been associated with the Creaton Church since 1972 and had rejoiced in the growth of the church in the intervening years. The churches of Castle Hill and Creaton have many historic associations and it was fitting for the gift to be made. The citation on an associated document reads:

'Presented to Doddridge & Commercial St. U.R.C. on Sept. 18th 1994 by their friends at Creaton U.R.C. in recognition of the long association between the two churches. Tradition maintains that this wooden travelling pulpit was used by Philip Doddridge on the occasions he preached on Creaton Village Green'.

Appendix 4:
Stages in the development of Castle Hill Church building

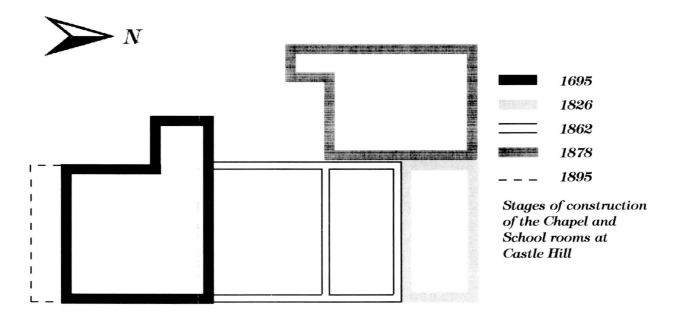

1695
1826
1862
1878
1895

*Stages of construction
of the Chapel and
School rooms at
Castle Hill*

Not drawn to scale

Based upon a plan by Roy Embrey